Normative Models in Managerial Decision-Making

by

Lawrence A. Gordon
Danny Miller
Henry Mintzberg

of
McGill University
Montreal, Canada

A study carried out on behalf of the
National Association of Accountants
New York, N.Y.
and
The Society of Industrial Accountants of Canada
Hamilton, Ontario, Canada

Published by

National Association of Accountants
919 Third Avenue, New York, N.Y. 10022
and
The Society of Industrial Accountants of Canada
154 Main St. E., Hamilton, Ontario, Canada
Copyright by National Association of Accountants ©1975
Copyright in Canada by The Society of Industrial Accountants of Canada ©1975
Library of Congress Catalog Card Number 75-21386
NAA Publication Number 7578

Foreword

This is our second release from a continuing research effort in the area of business decision models. The first release, *Impediments to the Use of Management Information,* authored by Henry Mintzberg, was published in January 1975.

The business decision models project, commissioned jointly by the Association and The Society, is an attempt to identify and interpret managerial information needs through a systematic examination of the decision-making processes. The project is concerned with the information which should be available ("normative study") and/or is actually available ("empirical study") in accordance with the managerial needs as they are presently perceived. The purpose is to explore the potential for developing a management accounting system designed to yield the information consistent with the decision processes and compatible with the organizational and individual patterns of managerial use of the accounting information.

The findings of the normative study presented in this publication will be followed by publications on the findings of the empirical studies within the project. It is expected that a report on the research methods in empirical studies of business decisions will be released for publication in the near future.

Special acknowledgments are due William L. Ferrara and John W. Ross for their gratuitous contributions beyond their respective advisory functions on the Project Committee. William L. Ferrara prepared the Lease-Buy Decision section for the report. John W. Ross practically co-directed the study.

We also are indebted to the referees who remain anonymous. Their suggestions were extremely helpful in preparing the revised draft of the report.

Guidance in the preparation of this report was kindly and generously supplied by the Project Committee:

William L. Ferrara (Chairman)
The Pennsylvania State University
University Park, Pa. U.S.A.

Norman J. Bell
Crown Cork & Seal
Don Mills, Ontario CANADA

James Don Edwards
University of Georgia
Athens, Ga. U.S.A.

Hadley P. Schaefer
University of Michigan
Ann Arbor, Mich. U.S.A.

John W. Ross
The Society of Industrial
    Accountants of Canada
Hamilton, Ontario CANADA

Calvin A. Vobroucek
Caterpillar Tractor Co.
Peoria, Ill. U.S.A.

The report reflects views of the researchers and not necessarily those of the co-sponsoring organizations or the Project Committee.

Stephen Landekich
Research Director
National Association of
    Accountants

Preface

This collection of nine frequently encountered decision models is in many ways unique. For each model there is a very successful attempt to capture the essential ingredients of the decision process as it was described in the normative (how should) literature. It was understood that the models would not necessarily describe management practice. The objective was simply to reflect the thrust of the normative literature via a brief introduction, a flowchart and a narrative description of each step in the flowchart backed up by a bibliography for each normative model.

The goal of the NAA/SIAC for this phase of the Business Decision Models research project was to present this collection of models to the business and academic community in order to encourage dialogue and discussion which could lead to:

1) improvements and/or refinements in the models plus suggestions for additional models to be researched.
2) empirical studies of each model in the real world in order to ascertain what adjustments (if any) might have to be made in the models under various circumstances in order to make them more meaningful and useful in the real world.
3) a greater appreciation of the data (accounting and otherwise) required to implement the models which could and should lead to improved accounting and other information systems.

An additional benefit of these studies of business decision models could easily be improvements in financial reporting and facilitating the resolution of financial reporting problems. For example, it can be argued that resolving the issue of how to report leases or mergers and acquisitions in financial statements is impossible without a firm grasp of decision models concerning lease-buy and merger and acquisition. It can be argued further that too few of those who propose resolutions to these two financial reporting issues have a sufficient grasp of the related decision model.

Thus the potential utility of this study could be greater than the utility of any prior NAA/SIAC research effort. Let the dialogue and discussion begin.

William L. Ferrara
Professor of Accounting and
Price Waterhouse Faculty Fellow
The Pennsylvania State University
Chairman of the NAA/SIAC
    Advisory Committee on Business
    Decision Models

Table of Contents

Normative Models in Managerial Decision-Making

Introduction

This study of normative models of managerial decision-making was initiated as part of the Business Decision Models research project which is intended to investigate how managers make use of information in decision-making. The study delineates some of the models of the most common managerial decision processes that have been postulated in the normative (or prescriptive) literature of accounting, management science, marketing, finance and organizational behavior. The Business Decision Models research project calls for a separate study which involves empirical (descriptive) research on actual decision processes in manufacturing firms, with the intention of analyzing the information actually used in managerial decision processes. A reconciliation will then be attempted between the normative and descriptive results in order to develop theories and hypotheses about how managers make use of information. It should, therefore, be emphasized that this study is not designed to stand alone but is to be coupled with the forthcoming descriptive study.

We should clarify our use of two terms at this point. A *decision process* is any interrelated set of activities leading to a "decision"—a commitment to action (usually a commitment of resources). A *decision model* is a decision process that is reasonably well-defined (outside the brain of the decision-maker, e.g., in flowchart form, in mathematical notation, on paper, or in a computer memory). In this paper we are dealing only with *normative* decision models—that is, those which are designed to *pre*scribe a desirable procedure but not necessarily to *de*scribe the decision process actually used.

Methodology

Our approach to the study of normative decision models was as follows. We began by extensively reviewing the periodicals and other literature across a wide range of fields. In all, about 40 periodicals were scanned for periods of publication ranging from two to ten years. From

1

this review, we listed all the articles we thought would be relevant (about 500) and, to a lesser extent, the appropriate books and monographs. The next step was to categorize each reference in terms of a decision type and, in effect, to produce a reasonably complete list of the decision processes that are treated in some detail in the normative literature of management.

We then selected from the list nine processes as candidates for detailed description. Our choices were based on two criteria: first, that the decision process was one commonly encountered in both the normative literature and the real world; second, that these choices would reflect a reasonable mix of the decision process common to a manufacturing firm, for example, at least one from each of the functional areas. We did, however, systematically exclude the lower-level, highly repetitive, and often fully programmed decision processes, such as those related to production scheduling and inventory control. Although these make up a large part of the normative literature, typically they are not decisions with which managers (as opposed to specialists, clerks or computers) concern themselves, and so we considered them beyond the scope of this study. The nine decisions we selected are

1. New Product Decision
2. Distribution Channels Decision
3. Acquisition Decision
4. Divestment (Product Abandonment) Decision
5. Capital Expenditure Decision
6. Make or Buy Decision
7. Lease or Buy Decision
8. Pricing Decision
9. Manpower Planning Decision

(The Personnel Recruitment Decision is shown as an appendix to the Manpower Planning Decision.)

For each decision process, we reviewed the literature and then developed a flowchart (or model) to capture the essential process prescribed there. We must emphasize two points here. First, these decision models were designed to reflect only the normative literature; they do not necessarily reflect management practice and are not statements of our own views of how these decisions should be made. Second, the models are designed to reflect the main thrust of the normative literature, not the best, the most detailed, or the most avant-garde of it. We did not try to represent sophisticated mathematical renditions of the models; rather we sought to describe the basic normative literature in a straightforward way.[1] Some of the flowcharts resemble two or three of the most appropriate flowcharts we found in the literature. In effect, where there was convergence on a standard model, we followed that line of thought. In other cases, we could find no flowcharts per se, and we then developed our own, taking into account the main line views presented. In all cases, however, the models represent our own attempt to synthesize these views.

Outline of the Report

In Section I we present an overview of normative decision theory and discuss the various types of decision processes that are treated there. In Section II we present some general (and normative) conclusions about normative decision theory—its orientation, its strength and gaps, and the directions in which it perhaps should go in the future. Then, in Section III, we present the nine models. In each case, the format is the same. After a brief introduction, we present the flowchart, which, as noted above, represents some synthesis of the normative literature. This is followed by a narrative description of the steps in the process, the information used, the sources of such information, and any standard techniques that are used along the way. (Note, however, that our focus is not on techniques but on decision processes; we show the techniques as they are used, but our intention is not to describe techniques per se.) Finally, attached to each model is a listing of the literature that we found in our search of the standard journals. These bibliographies contain simple and more rigorous items on the decision process and are, we believe, thorough but not necessarily comprehensive. The literature on normative decision theory is vast, and much of it is hidden in pockets which we did not find.

I. An Overview of Normative Decision Theory

The normative literature of management is reasonably unequivocal in its delineation of decision processes. Table 1 lists 37 decision process areas that are discussed there. But the clarity of delineation is misleading for it represents no more than the fact that at some point in time a

---

[1] Our approach raises the interesting point that our task was basically descriptive—to describe the normative models in the literature. Except in Section II, and the part of Section I dealing with decision types by output, we did not take a normative tack!

Table 1: List of Decision Process Areas
Discussed in the Normative Management Literature

Acquisition and Merger
Advertising
Asset Management
Capital Budgeting
Compensation of Manpower
Cost Allocation
Credit Granting
Distribution Channels
Divestment
Equipment Replacement
Financial Policy
Grievance Handling
Input Substitution
Investment
Labor Negotiations
Lease or Buy
Make or Buy
Manpower—Allocation and Planning
       —Performance Assessment
       —Recruitment and Selection
       —Training and Development
Market Planning
New Market and New Product
Plant and Warehouse—Capacity and Expansion
         —Design
         —Investment
         —Layout
         —Location
Portfolio
Pricing
Product Design and Planning
Production Planning
Production Scheduling
Purchasing
Quality
Research and Development
Structure

researcher defined some kind of abstract decision model, and other researchers subsequently followed up his line of development. Hence, there is a stream of papers on capital budgeting, on manpower planning, on lease or buy decisions. What is not clear in this literature, however, is how these decision processes interrelate in the world of organizations.

First, we may ask whether any or all of the decision processes exist in reality or if they are merely inventions of management science. Should we, as was suggested as an approach for descriptive study, focus not on decisions at all (since they are merely expressions of intention) but on events (such as the sale of a product) as tangible manifestations of managerial actions?[2] Second, assuming some processes do indeed exist in one form or another, we may ask what kind of overlap occurs. For example, how many processes—new product, plant investment, etc.—are assumed under capital budgeting? Where does one decision process end and the next begin? And perhaps most important, have decision processes been fully defined? The difference between determining a price for a new product and developing a manpower plan is indeed great. The former essentially involves a single choice; the latter entails many choices and much design activity. To conclude, we are struck by the lack of rationalization in the literature, by the fact that each decision process has its adherents and often they are unconcerned about the context of their decision processes either in the literature or in the reality of the field.

There are a number of popular ways to distinguish between decision types, such as:

by functional area:	production
	marketing
	purchasing
	research and development
	finance
	accounting
	personnel
by process:	programmed
	semi-programmed
	unprogrammed

---

[2]This idea was suggested by Stephen Landekich.

by level:	operating
	administrative
	strategic

Each of these is of some use, but after applying them to our list of processes, collectively we found them wanting. They simply did not go far enough to help in understanding how decision processes are distinguished and interrelated. Hence, we introduce an additional scheme:

by output:	selection
	scale
	schedule
	allocation
	design
	plan

Each of these categorization schemes and its relevance is described below.

Decision Models by Functional Area

It is relatively easy to categorize decisions by functional area. New product decisions usually are treated in the marketing domain, capital budgeting in accounting and finance, manpower planning in personnel, equipment replacement in production. In some cases there is clear overlap—product mix decisions cut across marketing and production, make or buy decisions across finance and production, and so on. But in general, we could fit almost all the papers in the literature into one of the four broad fields—production and purchasing, marketing and research and development, finance and accounting, and personnel.

The ease with which this can be done, however, should not imply that the categorization scheme is necessarily useful, for the neat categories may only reflect the abstractness of both the functional fields and the normative literature. Professors who call their field marketing develop new market decision models, just as organizational structure decision models are the domain of the organizational behaviorists. But the reality may be vastly different —for example, the production implications of new market decisions may be far more important to the general manager than to the marketing professor. Hence, we conclude that this first scheme is of limited usefulness and that the normative literature requires much consolidation across functional areas. Decisions must be viewed essentially as multi-functional (there is no such thing as a pure financial decision or a pure marketing decision) and there must be a recognition that sometimes different functional areas approach the same process from different viewpoints (e.g., new product decision models and acquisition decision models are two types of cost/benefit analysis).

Decision Models by Process and Level

These two categories overlap and may be treated together. Operating decisions, at the lowest levels of the organization, are often repetitive in nature and are, as a result, highly programmed. The normative decision models at the operating level reflect this fact, and indeed, many have been successfully implemented (e.g., production scheduling, inventory control.) As noted earlier, this report does not deal with these processes as they are not typically made by managers.

Strategic decisions, at the highest organizational levels, are often unprogrammed in nature. For example, the senior manager may have no preformulated procedures for dealing with major, one-time crises. If no such procedure for a decision process exists, then by definition there is no "model" for it. Hence, a number of crucial decision areas—crisis-handling, leadership, and so on—are excluded from this study. There have been, however, some recent attempts to describe and structure some of the complex programs managers use. Appendix A contains three examples of descriptive work—the information scanning program developed by Aguilar, the time scheduling program developed by Radomsky, and a general program for making strategic decisions developed by Mintzberg, Raisinghani and Theoret.

But somewhere between the fully programmed operating decisions and the non-programmed strategic decisions lies a series of decisions that are "semi-programmed." Models, or predetermined procedures, exist that specify *in part,* step by step, how they should be made. These semi-programmed decision processes may be made at the middle managerial level (e.g., pricing) or at the strategy level (e.g., new product introduction). Their key feature is that they are sufficiently comprehensible and repetitious so normative researchers have been able to structure them and prescribe models for making them. These semi-programmed models are the subject of this report.

It is imperative to note that semi-programmed may mean a variety of things, ranging from a relatively well-ordered set of steps, many perhaps involving precise mathematics, to a loosely ordered sequence of steps described only in general terms.

7

Decision Models by Output

It may be that decision processes are most clearly distinguished in terms of their outputs or the actions taken as a result of them. Many decision processes lead to the *selection* of a fixed course of action from among given, discrete alternatives (go, no go; A, B, or C; etc.). Make or buy and acquisition decisions typically fall into this grouping. A second group of decision processes leads to the choice of a point along a *scale*, that is, determining the level of a variable. Pricing decisions fit into this category. Third, there are decision models that deal with *schedule,* that is, deciding when a course of action will be followed. Replacement of equipment, for example, is treated in some of the literature as a scheduling problem—when to replace. *Allocation* decisions determine how a fixed set of resources will be allocated. Such decisions are encountered, for example, in budgeting models (capital or operating funds), in personnel (manpower assignment), and in marketing (allocation of salesmen efforts).

All of the decision processes above tend to focus on the evaluation and choice of alternatives. A very different set of processes deals not only with evaluation and choice, but also with *design* issues. These decision processes emphasize complex design in order to create new configurations (rather than simply to evaluate them). Typical design decision models deal with plant layout, organizational development and product design.

Finally, there are situations in which many decisions of all types are made in a single process. In fact, this is what we mean by *planning*—the making of clusters of decisions in systematic, integrated fashion. In this last category may be included market planning, production planning, R & D planning, manpower planning, facilities planning, and so on. Typically, each encompasses selection, scale, schedule, allocation and design decisions. For example, a marketing plan may cover what products to market, their designs, volumes, introduction times and advertising allocations.

To summarize this section: (1) we are dealing with decision models from all the main functional areas, and although most models fall clearly into one area or another, we suspect that the neat distinctions are somewhat artificial; (2) we are dealing exclusively with semi-programmed decision models at the administrative and strategic levels, the fully programmed models at the operating level being a different class and beyond the scope of this study, and the unprogrammed processes being, by definition, absent from the normative literature on decision models; and (3) our study encompasses decision processes with various types of outputs, including selections, scales, schedules, allocations, designs and plans. Table 2 shows a number of common decision types categorized by the functional areas in which they are usually treated in the literature and by their type of output.

II.   Some Normative Conclusions about the Normative Literature

In the next section, the body of this report, we are *descriptive* about the normative literature—describing it as it is. But in this section we shall be *normative*—prescribing how the literature should evolve.

From our reading of the normative literature, it appears that this literature can be grouped into two types. The *practitioner* literature derives from the experience of individuals, reflects a how-to-do-it (or more exactly, how-I-did-it) flavor, and is generally broad but loose and vague. The *management science* literature is typically more rigorous, but also more rigid and narrow. Our comments in this section pertain to the latter body of literature since this is the growing and currently more popular one and since this reflects the greatest hope for systematically improving organizational decision-making.

Below, we discuss a number of assumptions implicit (and sometimes explicit) in much of the management science literature. We do so with the full knowledge that, contrary to the assumptions, some of the literature does present quite realistic decision models and that there is a growing body of literature on information economics and other related issues which deals with these assumptions directly. Nevertheless, we feel that the assumptions discussed below do indeed reflect the general thrust of the normative models literature today. After discussing these assumptions, we draw a number of general conclusions about the directions in which the normative literature might go.

Implicit Assumptions

1.   *Decision processes are independent.*

In much of the normative literature (excluding that on planning), decision processes are treated in isolation. New product decisions usually are viewed as independent of capital gearing decisions which are viewed as independent of manpower recruiting decisions. Lease-buy

	Production and Purchasing	Marketing and Research Development	Accounting and Finance	Personnel
Selection	Lease or buy Make or buy Plant location Vendor selection Equipment acquisition	New product New market Sell or process further R & D project	Acquisition & merger Credit granting	Recruiting
Scale	Input substitution Plant capacity Plant expansion Purchasing Volume of production	Bidding Pricing	Transfer pricing Equity pricing Corporate objectives	Compensation of manpower Labor negotiation Workforce size
Schedule	Equipment replacement Project scheduling Production scheduling Inventory control	Media scheduling	Depreciation policy Write-off policy	Managerial time allocation

Allocation	Input substitution	Marketing effort Advertising budgeting Advertising media	Capital allocation Cost allocation Investment/divestment Portfolio selection	Manpower assignment

Design	Plant design
	Plant layout
	Production quality
	Facilities design
	Assembly line balancing
		Distribution channels
		Product design
		Promotion and
		    Advertising program
			Financial policy
			Accounting system
			MIS system
				Grievance handling
				Organization
				    development
				Organization structure
				Job design

Plan	Production planning Facilities planning	Advertising planning Market planning R & D planning Strategic planning	Asset planning Financial planning Short-term budgeting	Manpower planning

**Table 2: Some Common Decision Models
by Functional Area and Output**

decisions are treated independently of financial reporting decisions, so that in actual practice, as often contrasted to some normative models, firms are enticed into excessive lease commitments because they can avoid reporting them as liabilities in financial statements. Also, spill-over effects are seldom accounted for. We believe that managers deal with systems of decisions, that the decisions are interrelated in complex ways, and that managers are far more concerned with these interrela-tionships than are many of the normative theorists.

2. *Decision-making consists of selection from given alternatives.*

In many (not all) of the models, it is assumed at the outset that the alternatives stand ready to be evaluated. In fact, there has been repeated criticism in the descriptive literature that perhaps the most difficult aspects of decision-making precede evaluation—the diagnosis of the decision situation and the design and generation of alternatives. It is interesting to note that the most specific decision models in Section III deal exclusively with selection, and the most vague deal with design issues.

3. *All necessary data are available, at no cost, and are reliable.*

There is relatively little discussion of the availability of data, of their reliability, or of the costs of collecting them. (Recently these problems have been receiving attention, particularly in the accounting journals.) In fact, much of the called-for data often are unavailable or unreliable. For example, it is almost impossible in most situations to get reliable market demand data, and often such ordinary data as variable and fixed costs of a product are of questionable accuracy. The reliability of cost allocation schemes is often ignored in pricing decisions, while in capital budgeting and make-buy decisions, firms are dependent on cash flow rather than accrual accounting information. Often there is a need to rely on surrogate measures which may not accurately reflect the parameter to be measured.

4. *The organization can afford the models.*

In fact, some models call for data that cannot be collected except at exorbitant cost and require demanding computational techniques. Also, organizations sometimes are forced to make decisions under great time pressures (e.g., in crises situations), and here even the more simple techniques may be too slow.

5. *The models are useful in all situations and all organizations.*

The decision models often do not distinguish different situations, for example, small vs. large organizations (the former being unable to afford much analysis), public vs. private organizations (the former having more complex goal systems), competitive vs. monopolistic organizations, and so on.

6. *The organization consists of a clear hierarchy of authority with the decision maker at the top.*

Conflicts among decision makers, political pressures, bargaining, difficulties of implementation, and so on are simply not recognized in most of the literature. Implicitly, the models suggest that the results of analysis are fed up the hierarchy to one man who makes a "rational" choice which is then fed down the hierarchy for implementation.

7. *The organization has a clear and explicit goal system, usually the maximization of profits.*

The profit maximization assumption is probably the strongest assumption of normative decision theory. Perhaps it is made, not because the management scientist believes in profit per se, but because his models typically require an explicit, quantifiable (that is, operational) goal system, ideally consisting of a single measure. Profit fits these needs and is both legitimate and convenient. However, typical organizations have multiple and noncomparable goals, some of which are operational and others not. In addition to the economic goals are social, behavioral, legal and political goals. Organizations that are tightly controlled (e.g., an entrepreneurial firm) may be able to focus almost exclusively on economic goals. But those that are not (e.g., hospitals or business firms that experience great social pressures) must somehow deal with conflicting goals. The descriptive literature suggests that they may do so by sequential attention to different goals, by satisficing (treating goals as constraints and merely looking for acceptable solutions), and in other ways. But the normative literature largely skirts these issues, often paying lip service to noneconomic goals but doing little with them. At best it postulates a utility function in place of profit, but the clear evidence from the field is that managers simply cannot articulate general utility functions, even in relatively simple situations.[3]

8. *Decision-making takes place in a closed, static environment.*

Contrary to empirical evidence, most normative models make the implicit assumption that the decision processes are never interrupted with new information or new pressures, that there is no need to wait for feedback, that competition does not react to decisions while in progress, and that managers find no need to time the decision-making steps.

9. *Decision-making involves a fixed sequence of steps.*

The flowchart models especially reflect the notion of an inviolate sequence of events, but almost all the literature rests on this assumption. Goals are stated, information is collected, alternatives are evaluated, choices are made. In fact, there is clear empirical evidence that decision-making is much more of a circular process, wherein steps are intimately connected. One researcher addressed the ''phase theorem''—the notion of a fixed sequence of steps—and found that although distinct steps could be delineated, they were not sequenced in any simple or straightforward way.[4]

10. *Decision-making is a "once and for all" process.*

Another important assumption in the normative literature is that decisions are made once and for all in a single process. In fact, there is evidence from the field that high-level decisions span long time periods because they involve much groping and cycling behavior whereby the organization gradually crystallizes a complex issue. Information is gathered iteratively, and complex ''decisions'' are in fact split into series of subdecisions which are made one by one.[5] One major issue in the current descriptive literature is the notion of incrementalism in decision-making—that organizations move on big issues in small steps

---

[3]See, for example, D.O. Soelberg, ''Unprogrammed Decision Making,'' *Industrial Management Review* (Spring, 1967, pp. 19-29).

[4]E. Witte, ''Field Research a Complex Decision-Making Process—The Phase Theorem,'' *International Studies of Management and Organization* (1972, pp. 156-182).

[5]H. Mintzberg, D. Raisinghani, A. Theoret, *The Structure of ''Unstructured'' Decision Processes* (McGill University, Faculty of Management Working Paper, 1973).

in order to comprehend them. But the incremental view is simply not reflected in much of the normative literature. In fact, while the descriptive literature talks more and more of incrementalism, the normative literature talks more and more of planning—not just single decisions but great clusters of decisions made in integrated processes in single time periods. But despite their great popularity in the normative literature, the planning processes hardly have been studied empirically, and the few studies that have been published present discouraging results about their acceptance by managers.

Some Recommendations

1. *Normative decision theorists must carefully study the real world of decision-making.*

First and foremost, we see a need to reconcile descriptive and normative decision theories. We believe the onus is on the normative theorist to acquaint himself with descriptive reality—at the very least by reading the literature, at best by focusing more on the application of his models in the field. Often such arguments are met with the comment: current practice is no good; we must develop whole new approaches. But these whole new approaches are sometimes so detached from reality that they are useless. If dynamic factors, political pressures, non-operational goals, etc. are ignored in the models, how can the manager faced with these pressures make use of them?

2. *Normative decision models must encompass the whole decision process.*

The models must deal with problem recognition, diagnosis, design and generation of alternatives, and so on. There is an especially great need to focus on the ''softer'' parts of the process. These are of greatest importance to the manager even though they do not lend themselves to elegant modeling.

3. *There is a need to break down the functional barriers so that decision processes are viewed in the most relevant context.*

Decisions do not involve marketing, finance or personnel exclusively. The focus should be on the process and its needs, not on some artificial structure advocated by the business schools.

4. *The normative models must deal particularly with dynamic factors and multiple goals.*

Models must be developed for organizations with conflicting and non-operational goals and for situations of limited data, of timing, of interruptions, of delays, of cycling, of the gradual collection of information over time, of the factoring of larger decisions into smaller ones. In effect, we need *open-system* models of decision-making. This is especially so for decision models in the area of planning, where the time span of implementation is the greatest.

5. *Normative decision models should be designed on a contingent basis.*

There is a need for models that tell us that under conditions a, b and c, the path through the model should be x, y and z. When goals differ, when environments differ, when organization size differs, and so on, the model should reflect the need to do things differently.

6. *There is a need for standardization and integration in the normative literature.*

We found about 40 types of decision processes. And, typically, each is treated independently. But, in fact, there is room for definition of generic types—new product and acquisition decisions, for example, are basically selection-type decisions; organizational structure and plant layout decisions are essentially design decisions. Within each type we may be able to find standard subroutines (such as analysis of costs, generation of alternatives) which cut across the whole class. In effect, we should be working toward elaborating a system of standard normative subroutines, of a sophisticated nature, that are applicable to entire classes of decision processes.

III.   Nine Decision Models

As noted earlier, our nine models are all represented in flowchart form. This is one among many ways to show managerial decision models. We chose it for its clarity and simplicity. The models vary considerably from "soft" models (as in manpower planning decisions) to more rigorous treatments (as in pricing). This variation is meant to parallel the variations in the literature. Each model begins with a brief introduction, followed by the flowchart and then a narrative discussing processes and information used, sources of this information, and techniques used. Each model ends with a bibliograpy. Again, we must emphasize that these models represent a *description* of the *main thrust* of the *normative* literature. Thus, they do not reflect what we believe to be the right normative approach, nor are they necessarily the decision models actually used in practice. (Suggestion to the reader: It may be useful to review pages 1–17 after reading each of the nine models.)

Decision Models

New Product Decision

Introduction

There was much literature on how a firm should go about developing and marketing new products. The abundance of sources seemed to be matched by the amount of depth and detail most authors were able to devote to their discussion of this decision. The importance and complexity of this process would seem to account for these findings.

Some articles on the new product decisions were marketing oriented. Others focused more on the R & D and production aspects of the decision. A third group took the eclectic approach which is presented in the following pages. The flowchart shown was derived from several representative articles on the subject.

NORMATIVE MODEL OF
NEW PRODUCT DECISION

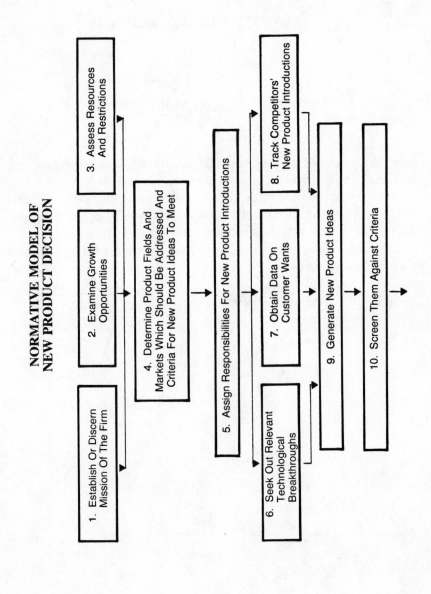

1. Establish Or Discern Mission Of The Firm

2. Examine Growth Opportunities

3. Assess Resources And Restrictions

4. Determine Product Fields And Markets Which Should Be Addressed And Criteria For New Product Ideas To Meet

5. Assign Responsibilities For New Product Introductions

6. Seek Out Relevant Technological Breakthroughs

7. Obtain Data On Customer Wants

8. Track Competitors' New Product Introductions

9. Generate New Product Ideas

10. Screen Them Against Criteria

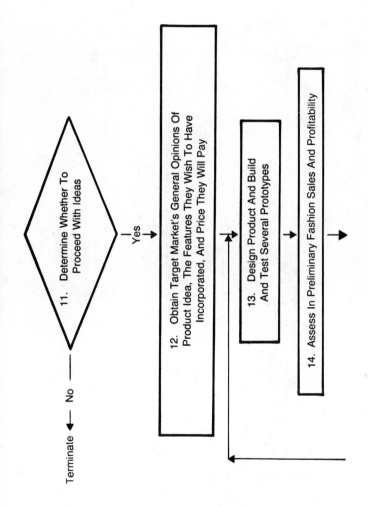

Terminate ← No

11. Determine Whether To Proceed With Ideas

Yes →

12. Obtain Target Market's General Opinions Of Product Idea, The Features They Wish To Have Incorporated, And Price They Will Pay

13. Design Product And Build And Test Several Prototypes

14. Assess In Preliminary Fashion Sales And Profitability

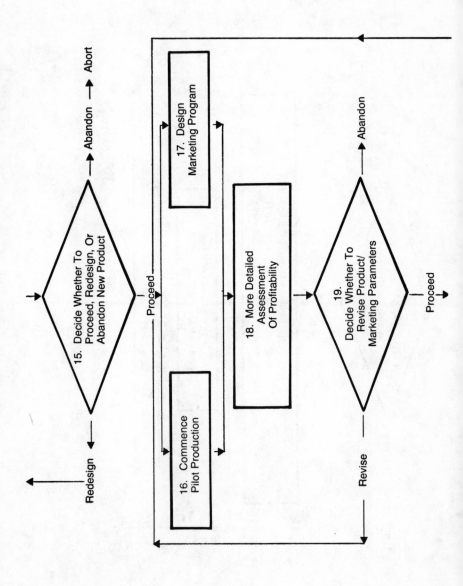

15. Decide Whether To Proceed, Redesign, Or Abandon New Product

Abandon → Abort

Redesign

Proceed

16. Commence Pilot Production

17. Design Marketing Program

18. More Detailed Assessment Of Profitability

19. Decide Whether To Revise Product/ Marketing Parameters

Abandon

Proceed

Revise

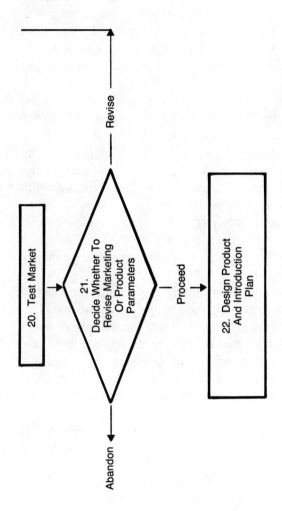

20. Test Market

21. Decide Whether To Revise Marketing Or Product Parameters

Revise

Abandon

Proceed

22. Design Product And Introduction Plan

Elaboration on the Flowchart

1. In introducing new products, it is important to have a fairly good conception of the *mission of the firm*. This can be clarified by discussions among top management (or owners) concerning the key organizational objectives and the basic business orientation which could most effectively accomplish these objectives. Once this has been accomplished, the firm has a much better frame of reference for assessing new product ideas.

2. The firm is then ready to examine in more detail the markets and product types which represent promising *growth opportunities*. To this end management may explore the types of products (their own and those of competitors) which seem to be highly successful. Also, the firm may search its own and other market segments or target markets in an attempt to discover those which are growing rapidly and include consumers with sufficient disposable income. A marketing team may examine the tastes of consumers in the more lucrative target markets by conducting surveys. Technical journals or trade papers might then be examined to elicit new product ideas which fit the tastes and capacities of the promising markets.

3. *Resources and restrictions* concerning new product introduction must be taken into account as growth opportunities are considered. This serves as an effective *screening* process which immediately excludes products and markets which are well beyond the reach of the firm in the light of its financial capacities, its technical expertise, and the production and marketing resources available. Looking at resources available also serves as a directive mechanism for identifying product opportunities which fit the competences at hand. Sundry staff and financial specialists employed in the various functional areas of the firm could provide information on resources and restrictions to those focusing upon new product ideas.

4. Steps 1 and 3 provide the key inputs for deciding the basic *criteria* which must be met by new products, while step 2 gives management an idea of which basic markets or *product types* seem most promising. The firm's management should be in a position (on the basis of their own analysis coupled with the input of staff expertise) to decide at this point such questions as:

- Should we look for new products or maintain the status quo?
- Should we remain in the same basic product lines and concentrate merely on small product modifications?

- To what extent can we pour resources into new product development?
- Should we do our own research and development?

5. Having decided whether to explore new product ideas further and the basic direction and scope of such exploration, the *problem should be handed to the experts* or other appropriate personnel. Top management should ensure that individuals with the required types of skills and knowledge will be accountable for the various stages of new product introduction. Care must be taken to include representatives from a wide variety of areas. *Authority for final decisions should be clearly defined* on the basis of: 1) a list which specifies product introduction procedures and steps; 2) an examination of personnel records to isolate those employees with requisite competence; and 3) an organization chart which portrays extant authority structures to be used in assigning new responsibilities.

6. Experts, relevant publications and professional meetings might be used as sources of *specific new product ideas* in a more intensive search directed within the confines of the scope, procedures and organization defined in steps 1–5. *Relevant technological breakthroughs* must be watched closely by persons responsible for the task.

7. Surveys should be used to define more exactly the *desires and characteristics of target markets*.

8. An important source of new product ideas may be *competitor product introductions*. These may be more useful than reports of technological breakthroughs in that their operability or feasibility has been better established. Sources of information on competitor activities may be newspapers, trade papers, trade association meetings, etc.

9. Steps 6–8 should culminate in a *listing of specific new product ideas*.

10. New product ideas should be *screened* according to specific financial, volume and goal congruence criteria established in step 4.

11. *Decide whether to proceed* with new product development on basis of step 10. If ideas seem viable, more specific steps should be taken to develop new products. If not, terminate the search process and/or go back to step 6 or 9 and start again.

12. In view of one (or a specific set of) detailed new product idea, survey the *target market's opinions*. Determine via surveys of consumers whether they seem interested, the price they are willing to pay, and the features they would like to have incorporated into the proposed product.

13. Have engineering, development and production experts *build a new product prototype* and test its soundness. Carefully record problems encountered, instances of failure to meet design specifications, and cost implications.

14. Using the data on costs and market potential determined in steps 12 and 13, forecast the *costs, revenues and profits* of the new product.

15. On the basis of the projection made in step 14 and the new product criteria which have been established, *determine whether to proceed* with, redesign or terminate the development of the new product. If the market is not interested in the product, perhaps the item should be abandoned. If production costs are higher than expected but it is felt they could be lowered via advanced production techniques, perhaps redesign is necessary. If projections indicate that all is well and that criteria are being met, proceed to the final stages of product development starting with step 16.

16. *Commence pilot production.* A model or facility should be set up to iron the bugs out of the production process. (Some of these were identified in step 13.) This will give management a better idea of the type of setting required for full-scale production.

17. *Design the marketing program.* Policies, procedures and structural arrangements should be set up to guide pricing, promotion, distribution and aesthetic aspects of the new product. There are many considerations to be taken into account in accomplishing this goal. For example, the firm may look to past experiences with existing products, actions of competitors, financial limitations, market/product characteristics, advice from marketing consultants, ad agencies, and so forth.

18. The facts gathered in steps 16 and 17 should be incorporated into the analysis carried out in step 15 (perhaps using Bayesian techniques as referred to in the Pessemier references) to *determine more accurately the viability of the project.*

19. Make the *decision regarding whether to proceed with test marketing based* on the profitability analysis performed in step 18. Process or product revisions may be necessary if profitability seems too low.

20. *Test market* product as a final attempt to gauge its success. Professional agencies could be called in to help accomplish this step.

21. Use the results of step 20 to determine whether to go ahead with *product introduction.*

22. If results of test marketing warrant it, prepare a *plan for systematic product introduction.* It should encompass considerations regarding: where and when to acquire production equipment, the amount of inventory to keep on hand, which markets to supply first, which plants to

produce the product in, terms of sale, etc. Guidance might come from past experience with similar products and the advice of internal and outside experts.

BIBLIOGRAPHY

Aaker, D. "Using Buyer Behavior Models to Improve Marketing Decisions." *Journal of Marketing*. Vol. 34:3, July 1970.

Atkins, R. and M. Hamberg. "Computer Model for New Product Demand." *Harvard Business Review*. Vol. 45:2, March-April 1967.

Bass, F. *et al. Application of the Sciences in Marketing Management*. New York: Wiley, 1968.

Bernhardt, I. and K. MacKenzie. "Some Problems in Using Diffusion Models for New Products." *Management Science*. Vol. 19:2, October 1972.

Cardozo, R., J. Ross and W. Rudeluis. "New Product Decisions by Marketing Executives: A Computer Controlled Experiment." *Journal of Marketing*. Vol. 36:1, January 1972.

Charnes, A. *et al.* "DEMON: A Management Model for Marketing New Products." *California Management Review*. Vol. 11, Fall 1968.

Clark, W. and D. Socton. *Marketing and Management Science: A Symposium*. Homewood, Ill.: R.D. Irwin, 1970.

Claycamp, H. and L. Liddy. "Prediction of New Product Performance: An Analytical Approach." *Journal of Marketing Research*. November 1969.

Foster, D. "Developing a Product Market Strategy." *Long Range Planning*. Vol. 2:3, April 1970.

Freimer, M. and L. Simon. "Evaluation of Potential New Product Alternatives." *Management Science*. February 1967.

Herrmann, C. "Managing New Products in a Changing Market." *Journal of Marketing*. January 1962.

Hess, S. "The Use of Models in Marketing Timing Decisions." *Operations Research*. Vol. 15, July-August 1967.

Keegan, W. "Multinational Product Planning: Strategic Alternatives." *Journal of Marketing*. January 1969.

Kotler, P. "Competitive Strategies for New Product Marketing Over the Life Cycle." *Management Science*. Vol. 12:4, December 1965.

Kotler, P. "Marketing Mix Decisions for New Products." *Journal of Marketing Research*. Vol. 8, February 1964.

Levitt, T. "Exploit the Product Life-Cycle." *Harvard Business Review*. November-December 1965.

Lipstein, B. "Modelling and New Product Birth." *Journal of Advertising Research*. Vol. 10:5, October 1970.

Montgomery, D. and G. Urban. *Management Science in Marketing*. Englewood Cliffs, N.J.: Prentice-Hall, 1969.

Montgomery, D. and G. Urban. "Marketing Decision-Information Systems." *Journal of Marketing Research*. Vol. 7, May 1970.

Nevers, J. "Extensions of a New Product Growth Model." *Sloan Management Review*. Vol. 13:2, Winter 1972.

Ozanne, U. and B. Churchill, "Dimensions of the Industrial Adoption Process." *Journal of Marketing Research*. Vol. 8, August 1971.

Penny, J., I. Hunt and W. Twyman. "Product Testing Methodology in Relation to Marketing Problems: A Review." *Marketing Research Society Journal*. Vol. 14:1, 1972.

Pessemier, E. and H.P. Root. "The Dimensions of New Product Planning." *Journal of Marketing*. Vol. 37:1, January 1973.

Peterson, R. "New Venture Management in a Large Company." *Harvard Business Review*. May-June 1967.

Pilditch, J. "Design as a Function of Marketing: How Marketing Research Influences Design." *Marketing Research Society Journal*. Vol. 11:2, 1969.

Reynolds, F. "Problem Solving and Trial Use in the Adoption Process." *Journal of Marketing Research*. Vol. 8, February 1971.

Sawits, M. "Model for Branch Store Planning." *Harvard Business Review*. July-August 1967.

Sellstedt, B. and B. Naslund. "Product Development Plans." *Operations Research Quarterly*. December 1972.

Shenneman, W. "Product Evaluation Using the Assigned Value Approach." *Management Accounting* (NAA). May 1968.

Silk, A. "Preference and Perception Measures in New Product Development." *Industrial Management Review*. Vol. 11:1, Fall 1969.

Toll, R. "Analytical Techniques for New Product Planning." *Long Range Planning*. Vol. 1, April 1969.

Twedt, D. "How to Plan New Products, Improve Old Ones and Create Better Advertising." *Journal of Marketing*. Vol. 33:1, January 1969.

Urban, G. "A New Product Analysis and Decision Model." *Management Science*. Vol. 14:8, April 1968.

Urban, G. "SPRINTER: A Tool for New Product Decision Makers." *Industrial Management Review*. Spring 1967.

Webster, F. "New Product Adoption in Industrial Markets: A Framework for Analysis." *Journal of Marketing*. Vol. 33:3, July 1969.

Distribution Channels Decision

Introduction

For the most part, the distribution channels decision was described by much of the normative literature in rather cursory fashion. This could have been because the nature of this decision varies so much from one firm to another. The need for generality seems to have detracted from the meaningful detail which might have been incorporated into more specific models.

As was the case for many decisions discussed, the literature varied along the dimension of how fundamental to get regarding the definition of basic objectives, target markets, etc. Some articles assumed these things had been established or were implicit in the decision. Others elaborated on these fundamental activities.

The accompanying chart echoes the simplistic approach which was found in most of the literature.

**NORMATIVE MODEL OF
DISTRIBUTION CHANNELS DECISION**

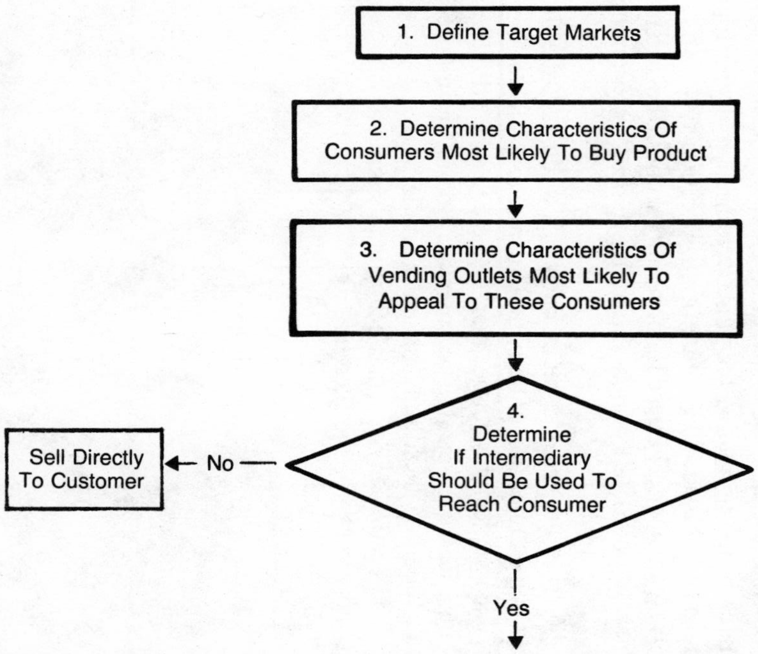

1. Define Target Markets

2. Determine Characteristics Of Consumers Most Likely To Buy Product

3. Determine Characteristics Of Vending Outlets Most Likely To Appeal To These Consumers

4. Determine If Intermediary Should Be Used To Reach Consumer

Yes

No

Sell Directly To Customer

34

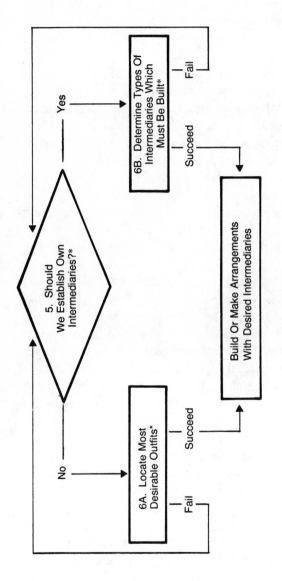

*Where specific analyses of steps 5 and 6A & B disclose an unfeasible situation, the decision maker must resort to the previous step.

Elaboration on the Flowchart

1. *Establish target markets.* Top management must, in the light of corporate objectives, the characteristics of its products (existing and anticipated), and the size, proximity, growth rates, and taste of potential consumers, select those target markets it wishes to focus upon. Many demographic data are available from advertising agencies, trade publications, marketing experts, etc.

2. Determine in detail the *buying characteristics* of the consumers who make up the selected target market. The incomes, ages, life styles, product tastes and buying habits of individuals in the target market should be established. This information enables the firm to determine the type of sales outlets which would most appeal to the consumers in question. Information on demographic factors can be obtained as per 1 above. More precise information about tastes and buying habits can be gathered via consumer surveys conducted by the firm or some professional agency. Questionnaires or interviews could be used for these purposes.

3. Establish the *characteristics of the most desirable outlets* in view of the analysis of results of step 2 above.

4. *Decide whether to use an intermediary* to reach the outlets defined in step 3. To make this decision, the manager must look at the potential number of consumers which could be reached with or without intermediaries. If historical data or projections supplied by distributors, ad agencies, published literature or corporate records disclose that a larger number of consumers can be reached via the use of intermediaries, a study of cost/benefits must take place. Intermediaries may affect profit margins through their influence upon: the effectiveness of order processing and quality of service; inventory levels and concomitant costs; shipping costs; packaging costs; and other potential overheads. Distributor estimates and accounting department historical data (on similar items and channels) and projections can supply information necessary to estimate the above items. If there is no appreciable difference in the number of consumers which could be reached with or without intermediaries, or if costs of intermediaries exceed the anticipated benefits to be derived, direct sales might be in order. If there is an advantage to be gained in using intermediaries according to the rough analysis which has been conducted, go to step 5.

5. *Decide whether to use own or outside intermediaries.* Step 4 provides the decision maker with a "rough" analysis of the costs and benefits of intermediaries, but now a more detailed estimate of inter-

mediary characteristics is required. The costs and benefits of using outside intermediaries should be compared with those of building one's own intermediaries. Present value and discounted cash flows can be used to assess the merits of investing in the building of facilities. It should be noted that steps 4 and 5 can be combined to yield a simultaneous analysis of three alternatives: use no intermediaries, use outside intermediaries, and build own intermediaries. If it is decided to use outside intermediaries, go to 6A. If it is decided to build own intermediaries, go to 6B.

6A. *Select the best among outside intermediaries.* Compare those establishments on the basis of: the number of desirable outlets reached and the size of the potential market; the quality of that market and the impact that selling to it will have on the image of the firm; the intermediaries' respective reputations for quality of service; their costs and charges (as per 4 above); and so on. Personal visits to intermediaries, an examination of the types of outlets which they service, and discussions with their clients (and ex-clients) will be useful in helping the firm with its problem of selection.

6B. Determine the specific *characteristics of intermediaries which should be built.* Consider such factors as budgeting limitations, appropriate locations (based on information gathered in steps 1 and 3 above), and optimal size and number of buildings. The last factor revolves around the trade off to be made between inventory storage and obsolescence costs and rental/overhead/construction and transportation costs. Inputs of information to estimate the costs and benefits may stem from quotes from builders, potential lessors, transportation companies, historical company records of inventory storage and obsolescence costs, etc. Present value and D.C.F. techniques could be used to increase the relevance of the cost-benefit analysis.

BIBLIOGRAPHY

Bowersox, D. "Planning Physical Distribution Operations with Dynamic Simulation." *Journal of Marketing*. Vol. 36:1, January 1972.

Bucklin, L. "A Theory of Channel Control." *Journal of Marketing*. Vol. 37:1, January 1973.

Collins, N. and L. Preston. "Analysis of Marketing Efficiency (Distribution Channels)." *Journal of Marketing Research*. Vol. 7, May 1966.

Hefferman, J. "Interaction in Product Distribution Systems." *Sloan Management Review*. Vol. 12:3, Spring 1971.

Hutchison, W. and J. Stolle. "How to Manage Physical Distribution." *Harvard Business Review*. Vol. 45:4, July-August 1968.

Kotler, P. *Marketing Management: Analysis, Planning and Control*. (Chapter 17) Englewood Cliffs, N.J.: Prentice-Hall, 1967.

Neuschel, R. "Physical Distribution—Forgotten Frontier." *Harvard Business Review*. Vol. 45:2, March-April 1967.

Rao, M. and S. Zionts. "Allocation of Transportation Units to Alternative Trips: a Column Generation Scheme with out-of-kilter Subproblems." *Operations Research*, Vol. 16, January 1968.

Smith, W. "Dynamic Program Model of Production—Distribution and Storage." *Journal of Industrial Engineering*. January 1966.

Acquisition Decision

Introduction

The literature on acquisition (merger) decisions is quite extensive and, for the most part, rather global in scope. For example, in many instances, there are discussions of the fundamental goals of the acquiring organization, analysis of its strengths and weaknesses, and so forth. Probably the far-reaching consequences of the acquisition decision are responsible for so broad an orientation.

No major discrepancies or "schools" could be found in the normative acquisition literature. Only variations in the emphasis of certain steps were noted. More specifically, some articles stressed the importance of a post-acquisition plan for integrating the new firm into the conglomerate, while others cursorily passed over this step. Some viewed assignment of responsibilities for the acquisition decisions as an explicit part of the decision, while others seemed to assume that this had already occurred once and for all.

The accompanying chart and write-up derives from the general nature of the information contained in the normative literature rather than any specific source.

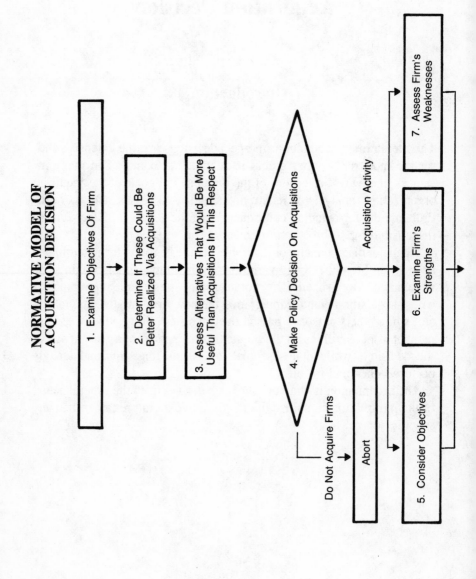

NORMATIVE MODEL OF ACQUISITION DECISION

1. Examine Objectives Of Firm

2. Determine If These Could Be Better Realized Via Acquisitions

3. Assess Alternatives That Would Be More Useful Than Acquisitions In This Respect

4. Make Policy Decision On Acquisitions

Do Not Acquire Firms

Abort

Acquisition Activity

5. Consider Objectives

6. Examine Firm's Strengths

7. Assess Firm's Weaknesses

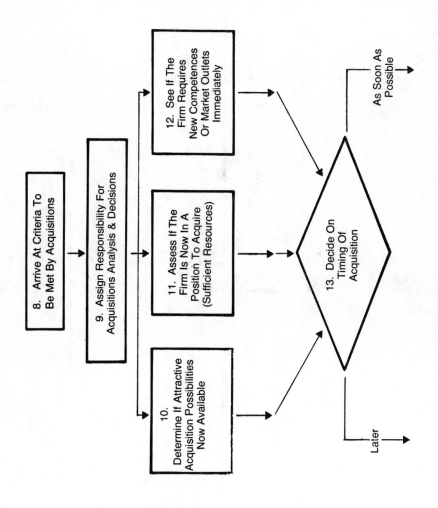

41

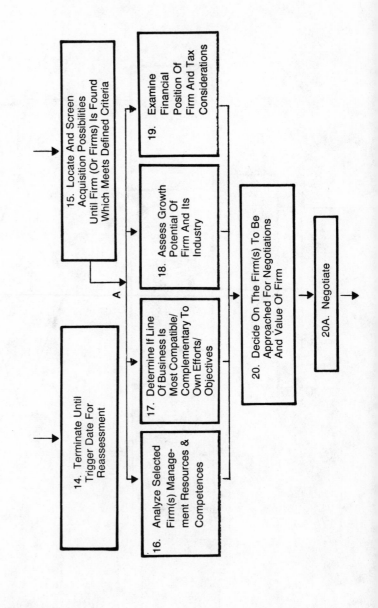

14. Terminate Until Trigger Date For Reassessment

15. Locate And Screen Acquisition Possibilities Until Firm (Or Firms) Is Found Which Meets Defined Criteria

A

16. Analyze Selected Firm(s) Management Resources & Competences

17. Determine If Line Of Business Is Most Compatible/ Complementary To Own Efforts/ Objectives

18. Assess Growth Potential Of Firm And Its Industry

19. Examine Financial Position Of Firm And Tax Considerations

20. Decide On The Firm(s) To Be Approached For Negotiations And Value Of Firm

20A. Negotiate

42

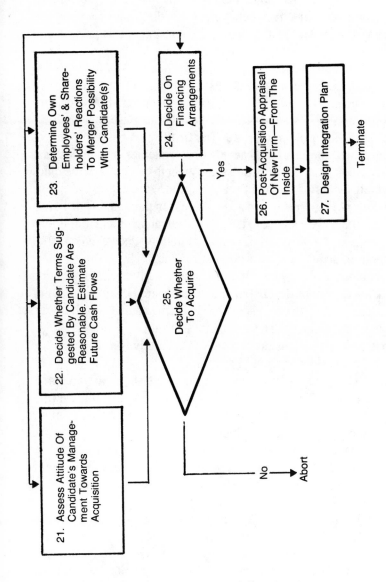

21. Assess Attitude Of Candidate's Management Towards Acquisition

22. Decide Whether Terms Suggested By Candidate Are Reasonable. Estimate Future Cash Flows

23. Determine Own Employees' & Shareholders' Reactions To Merger Possibility With Candidate(s)

24. Decide On Financing Arrangements

25. Decide Whether To Acquire

No → Abort

Yes →

26. Post-Acquisition Appraisal Of New Firm—From The Inside

27. Design Integration Plan

Terminate

Elaboration on the Flowchart

1. *Consider and define the objectives of the firm*. This step is essential since acquisitions should help the firm attain these objectives. The clarification of objectives can stem from discussions among top management and owners of the firm and should guide the acquisition decision.

2–3. *Establish the utility of acquisition as a basic tool in helping to achieve objectives*. For example, if it is the goal of a firm to grow in a certain area, acquisitions might be a useful tactic. If, however, immediate profitability is a superordinate goal, strategies other than acquisitions might be most appropriate. The firm's own past experiences with acquisitions, the results of acquisition strategies of competitors, and the advice of financial or acquisition specialists will provide clues on the overall merits of making an acquisition.

4. Make a *policy decision* on acquisitions. In the light of the firm's goals and its cursory research into the general advantages and limitations of acquisitions in terms of its financial situation, decide whether to further entertain acquisition as a potential tactic.

5. Set up broad *objectives* which pertain directly to the acquisition decision. That is, establish a list of the basic desired characteristics of acquisition candidates. Such a list may be constructed on the basis of the firm's marketing, financial and production resources and aspirations. Input about these aspirations may come from executive opinions, policy manuals, functional department heads, etc.

6. *Examine the firm's strengths*. Acquisitions should complement the firm's strengths. These might be assessed by establishing the products that are successful, the financial reserves of the firm, the unique skills available to the company which give it a particular competitive advantage, profitable market segments which could be exploited better via some acquisition, etc. The search and analysis necessary for carrying out this step can focus on financial statements, sales reports, marketing department appraisals of sales territories or target markets, and so forth.

7. Examine the firm's *weaknesses* and limitations using basically the same type of approach as that advocated in step 6.

8. Establish more SPECIFIC *criteria* which acquisition candidates must meet in the light of the objectives, strengths and weaknesses identified in steps 5, 6 and 7 respectively. For example, the firm might discover that a major weakness arises in the form of inadequate sources of supply, while a key strength is entailed by the technical expertise

presently on hand to set up efficient production processes. It might then become an objective of the firm to procure a company which produces the raw materials or parts required for its production process. Furthermore, if the firm has a product which is subject to cyclical market demand fluctuations, it may look for an acquisition candidate whose product's sales "dovetail" with its own. It is preferable that a list of such criteria emerge from the list of objectives, strengths and weaknesses evolved.

9. Top management should *assign responsibility* for analyzing and screening acquisition possibilities. It would be sensible to include individuals from a multitude of disciplines in a body that would deal with proposed acquisitions. If, for example, the prime purpose of an acquisition is, according to established objectives, to obtain a more useful marketing facility, the body should have strong marketing representation. Care must be taken to ensure that authority patterns as portrayed on the organization chart are not violated to any great extent in the acquisition analysis body's reporting pattern.

10. Determine if *attractive acquisition candidates* exist in the light of established criteria. This task should be performed by the acquisition group in consultation with investment dealers, financial report surveys, informal meetings with competitors, and so on.

11. Determine if the firm has sufficient *resources* to acquire the desirable acquisition candidate. A financial analysis must be undertaken to establish the repercussions of the acquisition on the present and projected asset, debt and equity positions.

12. It is important to determine *how urgently* the firm must acquire the candidate. For example, one may consider to what extent the firm requires a new product, market, management group, technical resource or whatever immediately or whether it can afford to wait awhile. Marketing, personnel, costing and interim financial reports can be used in deciding the urgency of the situation. Another key factor which may influence the advantages of immediate acquisition is the general availability of alternative candidates.

13. On the basis of steps 10–12, decide on the *timing* of the acquisition.

14. If it is decided to *defer* the matter, postpone investigation to a specific future date and recycle to step 10.

15. If it is decided to proceed as soon as possible with the acquisition, *locate and screen* several candidates. Using the sources cited in step 10, find acquisition candidate(s) and make a rough cut at deciding if pros-

pect(s) might be worthwhile to follow up on by comparing its (their) basic features with criteria established in step 8.

16. *Analyze in detail* selected candidate(s) focusing on its *management resources* and skills. Establish whether managers seem in tune with current trends in the industry. Find out if they have been competent in adapting their organization to its environment. Consider any special skills or technical knowledge which the candidate might have that could prove useful to the parent company. Information on these factors could be gathered by interviews with the management of the candidate and records of its past performance.

17. *Determine compatibility of candidate's orientations.* One can proceed, for example, by examining the determinants of market demand for the candidate's products (look for synergy in distribution channels and promotional efforts) or by regarding the benefits of increased economies of scale which might stem from a merger of production facilities, and so on. Marketing and production specialists in both the candidate's and one's own firm can provide insights on compatibilities.

18. Assess candidate's *growth potential* by examining the sales, profit and market growth rates of the firm and its industry. Financial and market forecasts prepared by impartial parties might be the best source of information.

19. Examine the *financial position* of the candidate by inspecting such things as current and debt to equity ratios, past and projected earnings, the state of capital equipment, etc. Financial statements and records and plant tours also would be useful in this respect.

20. *Decide on firms to be approached* and arrive at a preliminary estimate of a *fair price* to pay. The decision could be made by weighting the information considered in steps 16–19 in order of importance. Weighting can be accomplished by a group of individuals whose assigned scores are averaged in some manner. Each weighted dimension must receive a rating. Aggregate ratings can be prepared for each candidate being considered. Those candidates who do best should once again be assessed by experts on the acquisition team in order to establish a reasonable bid price.

21. *Assess attitude* of candidate's management towards acquisition. Determine if executives seem motivated to become part of a larger corporate endeavor by interviewing these people. If not, decide whether their reluctance will pose serious problems to a successful integration of the firms.

22. Find out if candidate is willing *to accept bid price*. Discover if candidate is willing to consider a price close to that offered. If not, find

out why. Decide if some rapprochement can be achieved.

23. Examine the *climate within own firm* to specific acquisition proposal. What do shareholders and employees think? Do their feelings represent an obstacle to a successful integration of the firms?

24. Decide on *financing arrangements*. Expert counsel should be obtained in determining the cheapest or most efficient method of financing the acquisition. Consider costs of debt and equity financing, legal restrictions, risks of alternative methods, long-term effects on earnings, etc.

25. Using the techniques and approach discussed in step 20, make the *decision* on whether to make the acquisition.

26. Perform *post-acquisition appraisal*. Go through steps 16, 17, 18, 19 and 21 again, this time obtaining an insider's view of the state of the new acquisition. This is essential for establishing the constraints and opportunities which must be considered in order to devise a plan for integrating the firms.

27. *Design integration plan*. Use information gathered in step 26 to design an approach for integrating where desirable the operations of the acquired and parent firms. Some key questions which must be answered are:

- Should we replace new firm's top management?
- Should we close down inefficient facilities (theirs or ours)?
- Should we combine similar production processes under one roof?
- Is it desirable to reorient distribution channels?

Expert personnel in functional areas must help perform such an analysis.

BIBLIOGRAPHY

Buckley, A. "Some Guidelines for Acquisitions." *Accounting and Business Research*. Vol. 1, Summer 1971.

Denholm, D. "Acquisitions and the Management Accountant." *Management Accounting* (NAA). December 1968.

Gonedes, N. and K. Larson, "Business Combinations: An Exchange Ratio Determination Model." *Accounting Review*. October 1969.

Heeley, R. "Acquisitions and Mergers—Management Problems." *Management Accounting* (NAA). May 1969.

Lancey, R. "PIE Analysis in Acquisition Strategy." *Harvard Business Review*. Vol. 44:6, November-December 1966.

Lister, R. "Financing an Acquisition." *Accounting and Business Research*. Winter 1972.

Malek, F. "Master Plan for Merger Negotiations." *Harvard Business Review*. Vol. 48:1, January-February 1970.

Rhys, D. "Anatomy of a Merger." *Accounting and Business Research*. Winter 1972.

Rockwell, W. "How to Acquire a Company." *Harvard Business Review*. Vol. 46:5 September-October 1968.

Stephens, A. "Merger/Acquisition Valuation Approaches." *Management Accounting* (NAA). April 1968.

Stern, L. "Acquisitions: Another Viewpoint." *Journal of Marketing*. Vol. 31:3, July 1967.

Divestment (Product Abandonment) Decision

Introduction

The literature on the product divestment (product abandonment)[6] decision was more sparse than that on the new product decision. This could be due to the fact that divestment is less in evidence in a business context than its opposite counterpart—perhaps as a result of the common emphasis on growth instead of consolidation. The articles reviewed for purposes of this study were remarkably consistent. They varied little in both scope and precise content. The dominant feature of the decision models focused upon was their emphasis on the definition of product abandonment criteria. The following chart and write-up reflect to a substantial degree most of the elements contained in the normative literature that was reviewed.

---

[6]Some authors have chosen the term divestment, others, product abandonment, in discussing this decision. The former is a more general sort of nomenclature which can refer to any form of asset divestment. Here we are concerned only with the elimination of products.

NORMATIVE MODEL OF
DIVESTMENT (PRODUCT ABANDONMENT) DECISION

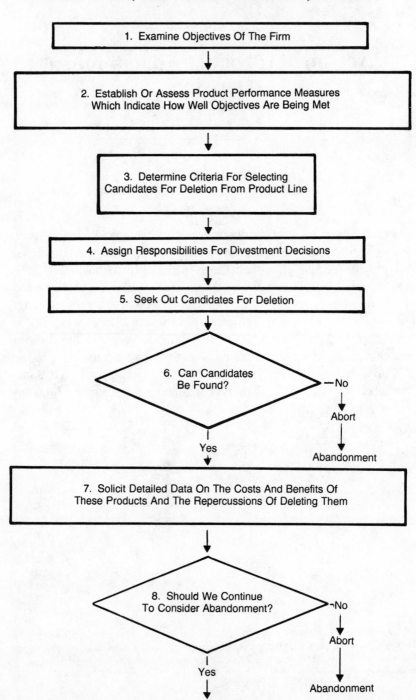

1. Examine Objectives Of The Firm

2. Establish Or Assess Product Performance Measures Which Indicate How Well Objectives Are Being Met

3. Determine Criteria For Selecting Candidates For Deletion From Product Line

4. Assign Responsibilities For Divestment Decisions

5. Seek Out Candidates For Deletion

6. Can Candidates Be Found? —No

Abort

Abandonment

Yes

7. Solicit Detailed Data On The Costs And Benefits Of These Products And The Repercussions Of Deleting Them

8. Should We Continue To Consider Abandonment? ¬No

Abort

Yes

Abandonment

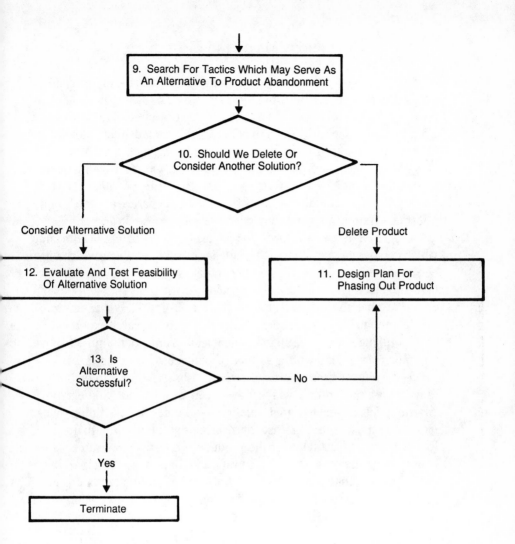

9. Search For Tactics Which May Serve As An Alternative To Product Abandonment

10. Should We Delete Or Consider Another Solution?

Consider Alternative Solution

Delete Product

12. Evaluate And Test Feasibility Of Alternative Solution

11. Design Plan For Phasing Out Product

13. Is Alternative Successful?

No

Yes

Terminate

51

Elaboration on the Flowchart

1–3. In view of the firm's objectives, *establish criteria for identifying products* which should be considered as candidates for abandonment. For example, if growth in sales is a key objective of the firm, then a product with declining sales may be considered a deletion candidate. On the other hand, if profitability is considered much more important than growth, then the firm may choose products which are losing money as deletion candidates. Information on goals can be obtained from management. Accounting and profit planning departments can supply information on sales volume and profitability.

4. *Assign responsibilities for divestment decisions.* Determine which persons are most knowledgeable in selecting products which must be eliminated. Personnel files or 'the grapevine' might provide information for selecting the persons best suited for the job. This will depend upon the objectives established in steps 1, 2 and 3. For example, if market growth is a key consideration, a marketing research expert would be a useful member on the abandonment team. A rule of thumb is to have a number of persons with a variety of perspectives on the team.

5–6. *Select candidates for deletion.* This selection is to be done in the light of the criteria which have been established. Some typical 'warning flags' which signal deletion candidates are declining sales, increasing manufacturing costs and shrinking contribution margins, a low return on investment for the product in question, consumer complaints about the product, etc. Naturally, the importance of any of these indicators is a function of the firm's objectives and its current state of health. Information to assist in candidate selection may stem from marketing and production records or reports and from customer communications.

7–8. *Perform detailed analysis of candidates.* Such an analysis must be performed to determine if resources could be more effectively used to accomplish objectives if several of the deletion candidates were dropped. The following issues might be dealt with:

- Determine if product is making money by examining accounting records;
- Consider whether another product could be produced in its place to make better use of resources;
- Analyze the potential effect of the deletion upon sales of other products;

- Calculate the impact of the deletion upon overhead expenses;
- Consider if displaced equipment could be sold or used for other purposes;
- Determine impact on the firm's cash position, labor force requirements, and company goodwill.

Information for carrying out each of these steps may be gathered by examining accounting records, marketing projections, cost studies, asset valuation and disposal experts, financial analysts, production and personnel department estimates, and customer opinions.

9. *Examine alternatives to product deletion.* Consider whether sales of the deletion candidate could be increased by more advertising, lower prices or design modifications. Consumer surveys and expert opinion from the production and marketing departments could help determine the merits of these alternative courses of action.

10. *Decide whether or not to delete product.* In order to ensure that as many key factors as possible have been considered in the foregoing analysis, circulate a checklist to various key personnel and have them list, weight and rate factors which should bear on the decision. The group making the final decision might find such an aggregation of expert opinion quite helpful.

11. *Design plan for phasing out the product.* Once it has been decided to eliminate the product, specific arrangements must be made to ensure smooth execution of the decision. Factors which may be considered are

- The time to halt production (it might be best to arrange this date so that it coincides with the start-up of new product production);
- The spare or replacement parts policy and the duration of time for which such parts will be available to customers;
- The disposal policy for old production equipment and the inventory of old products.

12–13. *Test feasibility of alternative solution(s).* Determine through further exploration and analysis of results, whether the alternatives proposed in step 9 have a reasonable chance of long-run success. If so, their implementation terminates the decision. If not, return to step 11.

BIBLIOGRAPHY

Alexander, R. "The Death and Burial of 'Sick' Products." *Journal of Marketing*. Vol. 28:2, April 1964.

Bettaner, A. "Strategy for Divestments." *Harvard Business Review*, Vol. 45:2, March-April 1967.

Hamelman, P. and E. Mozze. "Improving Product Abandonment Decisions." *Journal of Marketing*. Vol. 36:2, April 1972.

Hayes, R. "Optimal Strategies for Divestiture." *Operations Research*. Vol. 17, March-April 1969.

Hutchison, A. "Planned Euthanasia for Old Projects." *Long Range Planning*. Vol. 4, December 1971.

Kotler, P. "Phasing Out Weak Products." *Harvard Business Review*. March-April 1965.

Lewitt, T. "Exploit Product Life-Cycle." *Harvard Business Review*. November-December 1965.

Capital Expenditure Decision

Introduction

More has been written about the capital expenditure decision than most of the other decisions discussed in this report. Fortunately, there is some convergence of this literature, especially with respect to techniques. The portrayal of the decision presented here does not, however, attempt to cover all aspects of the problem, as that would require a separate report in itself. For example, issues such as ranking investments and dealing with multiple yields are not considered. Instead our flowchart illustrates *one general procedure and the most common techniques,* concentration on an individual investment with no capital rationing problems, of capital budgeting.

The model presented assumes stockholders' maximization as the firm's primary objective, which is consistent with most of the normative literature. Furthermore, it also assumes, as does most of the literature, that cash flows occur at discrete points in time.

NORMATIVE MODEL OF CAPITAL EXPENDITURE DECISION

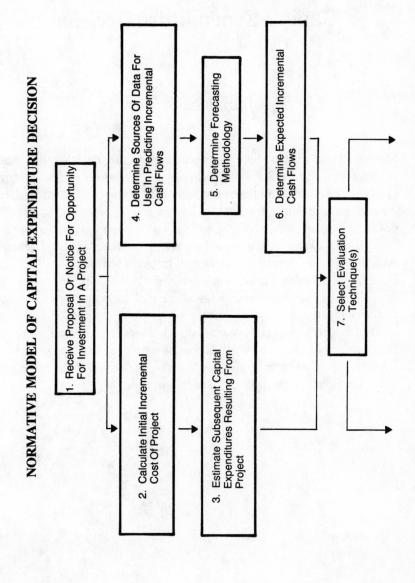

1. Receive Proposal Or Notice For Opportunity For Investment In A Project

2. Calculate Initial Incremental Cost Of Project

3. Estimate Subsequent Capital Expenditures Resulting From Project

4. Determine Sources Of Data For Use In Predicting Incremental Cash Flows

5. Determine Forecasting Methodology

6. Determine Expected Incremental Cash Flows

7. Select Evaluation Technique(s)

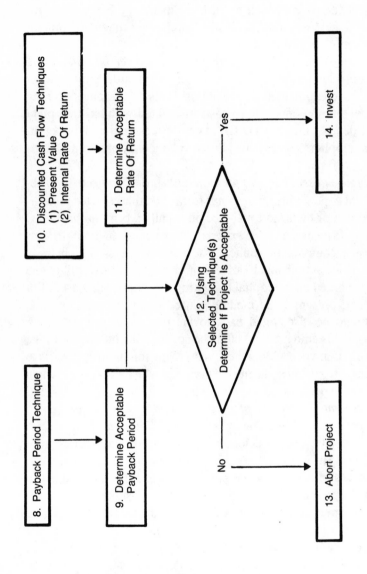

57

Elaboration on the Flowchart

1. *Proposal* or notice of opportunity for investment in a project is brought to management's attention. The opportunity could relate to any capital project (a project which has a life expectancy beyond the immediate period) such as plant expansion, purchase of major equipment, or development of a new product.

2. *Determine initial incremental costs of project by calculating cash and equivalent outlay for project.* The initial outlays may be for such things as equipment costs, building costs, additional working capital needs, and the opportunity costs associated with existing plant facilities needed for the project. Estimates of these items may be obtained from suppliers' price lists, historical records and expert estimates.

3. *Estimate subsequent capital expenditures.* The need for subsequent capital expenditures may result from such things as technological obsolescence or the need to replace physically worn-out machines. Estimates should be based on the expert opinions of production, marketing and cost accounting personnel. The periods during which these expected costs are anticipated to arise should be determined and treated appropriately, based on the capital budgeting technique being used. For example, if the present value method is used, then the expected cash outflows should be discounted back to the present to arrive at their present value. This amount would then be added to the initial cost of the project. An alternative to adding these costs to the initial investment is to treat them as cash outflows, during the period in which they occur, when computing the expected cash flows in step 6.

4–5. *Determine sources of data and techniques to be used in predicting incremental cash flows.* For example, internal financial records might be analyzed to determine past data on cash flows from similar projects. The accrual accounting information must, however, be converted to cash flow data since predicted cash flows are needed in determining the project's acceptability. Potential consumers and/or customers might represent other sources of cash flow information. These individuals could be surveyed in order to estimate the demand for the product which will be produced by the project in question. Also, marketing personnel may be able to provide some estimates on cash flows, which might serve as a check on information supplied by customers. Production and R & D department estimates may provide insight into projected technological trends and the life span of equipment to be used. Suppliers also could provide valuable cash flow data on anticipated operating costs. If the company has a forecasting department (or group) it will probably play an important role in determining the expected cash flows. Where feasible, quantitative as well as qualitative forecasting models should be utilized. Finally, tax accounting experts should be consulted to provide estimates of the tax impact upon cash flows.

6. *Determine expected cash flows.* Based on the data derived in steps 4 and 5, probability distributions of cash flows could be determined. From these distributions, the expected mean value of the cash flows for each period could be ascertained. These estimates could include an adjustment for risk which would result in the determination of the "certainty equivalent" cash flow. A risk adjustment usually is considered to be a function of the variance of the distribution of cash flows. In the more recent normative literature, utility theory and simulation techniques have been used for adjusting cash flows for risk. On the other hand, the adjustment for a project's risk could be accomplished by other means, such as using a "risk adjusted rate of return" or using a shorter payback period. (These points will be discussed further in steps 7, 8 and 11.)

7. *Select evaluation technique(s).* Various methods exist for evaluating capital projects. Among the most popular techniques advocated in the normative literature are: (1) present value, (2) internal rate of return, and (3) simple payback period.[7] The first two of these consider the time value of money and may be referred to as "discounted cash flow" (DCF) techniques. (In some of the literature, the term DCF is reserved for the present value method only.) The third method, the simple payback period, does not consider the time value of money.

The theoretical virtues of discounted cash flow techniques are well documented in the normative literature. On the other hand, the payback period method also has received some strong normative support, at least as a constraint if not as a criterion, as a means of reducing the uncertainty surrounding the capital budgeting decision. Thus it is often advocated that firms use both a DCF method and the payback period method in evaluating a capital project (i.e., follow steps 8 and 9, as well as steps 10 and 11).

Many capital projects are "must" projects. In these cases the decision to accept or reject a project is a *"fait accompli."* Therefore, this type of project does not require a capital budgeting decision in the traditional framework, and the normative literature does not usually treat it as such.

---

[7]There is also a discounted payback period.

Accordingly, our flowchart does not consider projects of this sort.

8. *Payback period technique.* A project's payback period, T, can be determined as follows:

$$\sum_{i=1}^{T} R_i = \text{Cost of Project}$$

where, $R_i = i$th period
net cash flow

Some factors which may sway a company in the direction of using the payback period method for evaluating a capital project are its ease of use, management's concern for the firm's liquidity, and management's confidence (or lack of confidence) in the estimate of the project's cash flows. For example, if a project has a high risk of becoming obsolete through technological advances, a firm may be well advised to consider, at least as a supplementary constraint to DCF information, the project's payback period.

9. *Determine acceptable payback period.* The normative literature is not abundant on procedures for determining an acceptable payback period for a project. The discussions which do appear on this topic seem to focus either on "managerial rules of thumb" which have evolved in practice (e.g., any project taking more than four periods to repay itself should, under normal circumstances, be rejected), or on the reciprocal of the payback period as an approximation of the IRR (e.g., if a project has cash flows which are approximately constant from period to period, then as long as the economic life of the project is at least twice the payback period, the payback reciprocal is a reasonable approximation to the project's internal rate of return). The one assumption that does, however, come through in the literature is that the shorter the estimated payback period, the lower the risk involved in the project.

10. *Discounted Cash Flow techniques.* The two capital budgeting methods most often advocated in the normative literature are: (a) the present value (PV) method, and (b) the internal rate of return (IRR) method. The present value of a project can be expressed algebraically:[8]

$$PV = \sum_{i=1}^{n} \frac{R_i}{(1+K)^i} + \frac{S}{(1+K)^n}$$

---

[8]A common alternative formulation is:

$$\text{Net Present Value} = NPV = \sum_{i=1}^{n} \frac{Ri}{(1+k)^i} + \sum_{i+1}^{n} \frac{Si}{(1+k)^i} - \sum_{i=0}^{n} Ci; \begin{bmatrix} NPV \geq 0, \text{ Accept} \\ NPV < 0, \text{ Reject} \end{bmatrix}$$

where,

R_i = net incremental cash flow
for period i

K = discount factor, which is
equal to the firm's minimum
acceptable rate of return

n = economic life of asset

S = salvage value of asset

In terms of a decision rule, if the present value (PV) of a project is greater than its cost (C), the project is desirable. On the other hand, if the present value (PV) is less than the project's cost (C), the project is undesirable. Lastly, if the project's present value (PV) equals its cost (C), the firm will be indifferent to the project.

The internal rate of return (IRR) method can be expressed algebraically as follows:

$$C = \sum_{i=1}^{n} \frac{R_i}{(1+IRR)^i} + \frac{S}{(1+IRR)^n}$$

where,

C = cost of project

R_i, n, S = same as above

In terms of a decision rule, if the IRR of a project (which has to be solved for in the above equation) is greater than the firm's minimum acceptable rate of return (K), the project is desirable. On the other hand, if the IRR of a project is less than the firm's minimum acceptable rate of return (K), the project is undesirable. Lastly, if the IRR of a project is equal to the firm's minimum acceptable rate of return (K), the firm will be indifferent to the project.

Both formulations given above assume cost (C) occurs in the current period (i=o) and S occurs in the last period (i=n), and that any C_i or S_i that occurs in other periods (i≠o for C_i and i≠n for S_i) is included in R_i.

11. *Determine acceptable rate of return.* The ''acceptable rate of return,'' often called the ''cost of capital,'' is the minimum rate a project must earn in order to cover the cost of funds to the firm. According to the bulk of the normative literature, companies have access to three sources of financing. These sources are debt (including leases), internal equity and external equity. Broadly speaking, the cost of capital can be computed as either a marginal cost from individual sources or as an average cost of capital from all of the three sources. The theoretical

literature seems to favor use of the average cost of capital, computed according to the firm's optimal capital structure. Cost of capital estimates may reflect the risk involved in the particular project, as well as the risks associated with financing, unless this risk has been fully considered in step 6. Investment at a firm's cost of capital, properly computed, should maintain the market value of the firm.[9]

Whether the "acceptable rate of return" is computed based on some optimal capital structure or some alternative approach, the normative literature does appear to converge on the idea that it must be adjusted for risk (unless risk has been *fully* accounted for elsewhere, e.g., in step 6). Thus, we might say that the thrust of the literature is to use a "risk-adjusted rate of return" in the DCF methods of capital expenditure analysis.

12–14. These are action steps which follow from the above analysis.

---

[9]Some of the most recent normative literature on capital budgeting suggests the use of the "capital asset pricing model" (CAPM) approach, which is based on capital markets and portfolio theory, to determine the cost of capital used in the DCF methods of capital budgeting. According to this model, the cost of capital for a project is equal to:

$$R_F + \beta_i [E(R_M) - R_F]$$

where,

R_F = risk-free rate

β_i = risk coefficient for asset i (i.e. the systematic risk for asset i)

$E(R_M)$ = expected return on market index

The assumptions necessary to apply the CAPM approach to capital budgeting decisions are quite stringent, and thus much disagreement still exists on its utility.

BIBLIOGRAPHY

Anderson, H. and R. Schwartz. "The Capital Facility Decision." *Management Accounting* (NAA). February 1971.

Anderson, L., V. Miller and S. Josephs. "Abstract: A Probability Distribution of Discounted Payback for Evaluation Investment Decisions." *Journal of Financial and Quantitative Analysis*. Vol. 7, March 1972.

Anderson, L. and V. Miller, "Capital Budgeting: A Modified Approach to Capital Allocation." *Management Accounting* (NAA). March 1969.

Ball, R. and P. Brown. "Portfolio Theory and Accounting." *Journal of Accounting Research*. Autumn 1973.

Bierman, H. "The Implications to Accounting of Efficient Markets and The Capital Asset Pricing Model." *The Accounting Review*. July 1974.

Bierman, H. and S. Smidt. "Capital Budgeting and the Problem of Reinvesting Cash Proceeds." *Journal of Business*. October 1957.

Bierman, H. and S. Smidt. *The Capital Budgeting Decision*. Third Edition. New York: The Macmillan Company, 1971.

Birnberg, J., L. Pondy and C. Davis. "Effect of Three Voting Rules on Resource Allocation Decision." *Management Science*. Vol. 16:6, February 1970.

Budd, A. and R. Litzenberger. "Corporate Investment Criteria and the Valuation of Risk Assets." *Journal of Financial and Quantitative Analysis*. Vol. 15, December 1970.

Burkert, Ronald L. "Recognizing Inflation in the Capital Budgeting Decision." *Management Accounting* (NAA). November 1971.

Chambers, J. and S. Mullick. "Investment Decision Making in a Multinational Enterprise." *Management Accounting* (NAA). August 1971.

Clarke, L. "Simulation in Capital Investment Decisions." *Journal of Industrial Engineering*. October 1968.

Cotton, F. "Profit Improvements Through Investment Decisions." *Journal of Industrial Engineering*, Annual Proceedings 19, 1968.

Dyckman, T. R. "Allocating Funds to Investment Projects When Returns Are Subject to Uncertainty: A Comment." *Management Science*. Vol. 11:3, November 1964.

Edge, C. G. *A Practical Manual on the Appraisal of Capital Expenditure*. Special Study #1, Revised Edition. The Society of Industrial and Cost Accountants of Canada, 1964.

Edwards, J. B. "Adjusted DCF Rate of Return." *Management Accounting* (NAA). January 1973.

Elnicki, R. "ROI Simulations for Investment Decisions." *Management Accounting* (NAA). February 1970.

English, J. "Economic Comparison for Engineering Projects." *Journal of Industrial Engineering*. November-December 1961.

Fanning, J. "How to Improve Investment Decisions." *Harvard Business Review*. Vol. 44:1, January-February 1966.

Ferrara, W. "Capital Budgeting and Financing or Leasing Decisions." *Management Accounting* (NAA). July 1968.

Fogler, R. "Ranking Techniques and Capital Budgeting." *The Accounting Review*. January 1972.

Foster, N. "New Ways to Analyze Capital Investments." *Journal of Industrial Engineering*. August 1971.

Fremgen, J. M. "Capital Budgeting Practices: A Survey." *Management Accounting* (NAA). May 1973.

Gerwin, D. "Compensation Decisions in Public Organizations." *Industrial Relations*. Vol. 7, February 1969.

Gordon, L. A. and M. C. Findlay. "IRR Computation and the Multi-Asset Problem." *Omega*. August 1974.

Greer, W. "Capital Budgeting Analysis with Timing of Events Uncertain." *The Accounting Review*. January 1970.

Hastings, N. "Resource Allocation in Project Networks." *Operations Research Quarterly*. Vol. 23, June 1972.

Hetrick, J. "A Formal Model for LRP: Allocating and Appraising Capital Investment." *Long Range Planning*. Vol. 2, September 1969.

Hillier, F. S. "The Derivation of Probabilistic Information for the Evaluation of Risky Investments." *Management Science*. Vol. 9:8, April 1963.

Jensen, M. and J. Long. "Corporate Investment Under Uncertainty and Pareto Optimality in the Capital Markets." *Bell Journal of Economics and Management Science*. Vol. 3, Spring 1972.

Juris, H. "Union Crisis Wage Decisions." *Industrial Relations*. Vol. 7, May 1969.

Klammer, T. "Empirical Evidence of the Adoption of Sophisticated Capital Budgeting Techniques." *Journal of Business*. July 1972.

Lamper, J.C. "The Trend Toward Automated Capital Investment Decisions." *Management Accounting* (NAA). April 1971.

Lusk, E. "Capital Investment Decision." *Accounting and Business Research*. Vol. 2, Autumn 1972.

Meredith, J. "Accounting and Contribution to the Selection of Business Investment." *Management Accounting* (NAA). April 1968.

National Association of Accountants. "Digest of NAA Research Report #43—Financial Analysis to Guide Capital Expenditure Decisions." *Management Accounting* (NAA). September 1967.

Petrovic, R. "Optimization of Resource Allocation in Project Planning." *Operations Research*. Vol. 16, May-June 1968.

Salazar, R. and S. Sen. "A Simulation Model of Capital Budgeting Under Uncertainty." *Management Science*. Vol. 15:4, December 1968.

Sharpe, W. "Capital Asset Prices: A Theory of Market Equilibrium Under Conditions of Risk." *The Journal of Finance*. September 1964.

Spier, L. "A Suggested Behavioral Approach to Cost-Benefit Analysis." *Management Science*. Vol. 17:10, June 1971.

Sundem, G. "Evaluating Simplified Capital Budgeting Models Using Time-state Preference Metric." *The Accounting Review*. April 1974.

Taylor, I. "Criteria for Selecting Proposals." *Journal of Industrial Engineering*. Annual Proceedings 22, 1971.

Tilles, S. "Strategies for Allocating Funds." *Harvard Business Review*. Vol. 44:1, January-February 1966.

Van Horne, J. "Capital Budgeting Decisions Involving Combinations of Risky Investments." *Management Science*. Vol. 13:2, October 1966.

Vernon, T. H. "Capital Budgeting and the Evaluation Process." *Management Accounting* (NAA). October 1972.

Weingartner, H. M. *Mathematical Programming and the Analysis of Capital Budgeting Problems*. Ford Foundation Doctoral Dissertation Winner. Englewood Cliffs, N.J.: Prentice-Hall, Inc., 1963.

Weingartner, H. M. "Some New Views on the Payback Period and Capital Budgeting Decisions." *Management Science*. Vol. 15:12, August 1969.

Wilson, R. "Investment Analysis under Uncertainty." *Management Science*. Vol. 15:12, August 1969.

Lease-Buy Decision[10]

Introduction

The lease-buy decision as portrayed in the normative literature is really a financing decision; i.e., it is considered only after a decision to invest has been made. Basically the computational procedure involves a determination of whether or not the cost or borrowing is more expensive than the implicit cost of leasing. Usually the lease is more expensive since a lease involves avoiding various risks of ownership for which a price must be paid. The real decision is whether or not the extra cost entailed in leasing is worth paying in order to avoid various risks of ownership.

A major impediment to sound lease-buy decisions is the unresolved issue of reporting lease commitments in financial statements. As long as prospective lessees can avoid reporting lease commitments as liabilities, they may be enticed into excessive lease commitments.

---

[10](This normative decision model was developed by W.L. Ferrara for this report.)

NORMATIVE MODEL OF LEASE-BUY DECISION

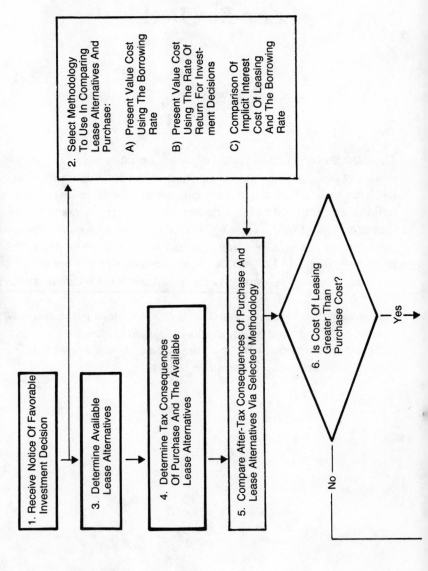

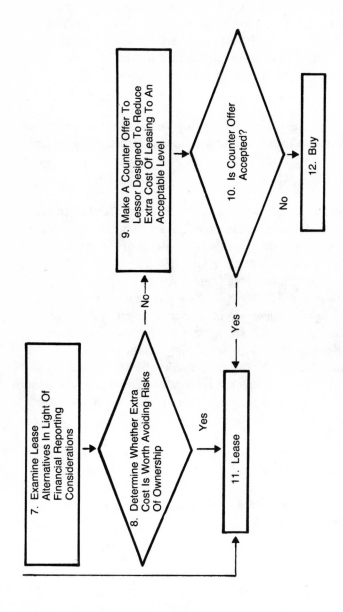

7. Examine Lease Alternatives In Light Of Financial Reporting Considerations

8. Determine Whether Extra Cost Is Worth Avoiding Risks Of Ownership

9. Make A Counter Offer To Lessor Designed To Reduce Extra Cost Of Leasing To An Acceptable Level

No

Yes

10. Is Counter Offer Accepted?

No

Yes

11. Lease

12. Buy

69

Elaboration on the Flowchart

1. As in Capital Expenditure Decision write-up.

2. The three basic methodologies compare the after-tax cash flows of each lease alternative with the after-tax cash flows of the purchase alternative. In each case the discounted cash flow technique is used. The three methodologies can be described briefly as follows:

a) Determine the annual after-tax cash flows of leasing and purchase, and then discount the two sets of cash flows at the lessee's after-tax cost of borrowing to determine the present value cost of each alternative.

b) Subtract from the annual lease flows the lessee's cost of borrowing to determine that portion of the lease flows which is the equivalent of the depreciation deduction. Discount the annual lease flows at the lessee's borrowing rate to determine the equivalent purchase price of the lease. Subtract the present value, using the rate of return for investment decisions, of the equivalent depreciation tax shield from the equivalent purchase price to determine the present value cost of leasing and compare this to the present value cost of purchase determined by subtracting the present value (using the same discount rate) of the depreciation tax shield from the purchase price. This methodology converts the lease into an investment decision which thus makes it appropriate to discount at the investment rate.

c) Determine the annual after-tax cash flows of leasing and purchase as in (a) above, and find the rate of discount which equates the present value of the two sets of flows. This rate of discount is the after-tax rate of interest implicit in leasing; it should be compared to the lessee's after-tax borrowing cost.

3. Available lease alternatives may be stated in published form along with prices for cash purchase and installment purchase by the lessor (manufacturer or distributor). In some instances lease alternatives may be determined through a process of negotiation with a financial institution. In all instances there appears to be room for negotiation between lessee and lessor concerning many facets of the lease contract

such as renewal provisions, purchase options, maintenance contracts, etc.

4. Since a lease which is "true" for income tax purposes will involve a different set of income tax deductions than a purchase, all lease-buy evaluations must be considered in terms of after-tax cash flows. Additional tax complications may enter the picture when leased and purchased assets are treated differently for tax purposes at the state or province and local level.

5. Great care must be exercised when comparing the after-tax consequences of purchase and lease alternatives. The alternatives must be comparable, or they must be made comparable. For example:

- A five-year lease commitment cannot be compared to the purchase of an asset with a 10-year economic life unless either a five-year lease renewal privilege is added to the lease alternative or the purchased asset is assumed to have a five-year economic life via resale of the purchased asset at its estimated salvage value at the end of five years.
- The estimated costs of maintenance must be added to the purchase cost (or subtracted from the lease rentals) when maintenance of leased equipment is covered by lease rentals.

6. Depending on the methodology used, the difference between lease and purchase cost is measured in terms of present values or interest rates. Either way, the lease usually should be more expensive since it enables the lessee to avoid ownership risks which the lessor assumes.

In those relatively uncommon situations when a lease is less expensive, an alternative to leasing could be a counter offer to the lessor involving a reduced purchase price. An interest rate implicit in leasing which is less than the lessee's borrowing rate is prima facie evidence of an inflated purchase price.[11]

7. The method of reporting lease commitments in financial statements can have a significant impact upon management's decision to lease or buy. Ability to report lease commitments via generalities in footnotes to financial statements and thus avoid treating such commitments as balance sheet liabilities can easily entice managements into

---

[11]A leveraged lease should be considered a special case in which the after-tax interest rate implicit in the lease could be lower than the lessee's borrowing rate.

overly expensive lease arrangements. It has been said that a great impetus toward lease financing in recent years has been the ability to generate "off balance sheet financing." The problem from a decision model point of view can be described in terms of "financial statement window dressing" tending to preclude the implementation of sound economic decisions.

8. The determination of whether the extra cost of leasing is a reasonable price to pay for avoiding various ownership risks can only be made subjectively. The specific risks (e.g., obsolescence of equipment or uncertain market for the product) to be avoided should be quantified insofar as possible to facilitate this determination. Inevitably intertwined in this admittedly subjective area is the ability to generate "off balance sheet financing" via leasing as mentioned above.[12]

9-10. If the extra cost of leasing is not worth incurring considering the ownership risks to be avoided, it is sensible for the lessee to make a counter offer to the lessor. The recognition of such counter offers makes it possible to consider negotiating a tailor-made leasing contract which matches taking on or avoiding various ownership risks at a price agreeable to the lessee and lessor. The negotiations must consider tax consequences, and they will inevitably consider financial reporting consequences.

11-12. The action steps which flow inevitably from all of the preceding evaluations and negotiations.

---

[12]If the after-tax interest rate implicit in the lease is approximately equal to or greater than the lessee's minimum desired after-tax return for investment decisions, the lessee should consider re-examining his investment decision before leasing.

BIBLIOGRAPHY

Aly, H. "The Lease or Buy Decision: An Opportunity Cost Approach." *Cost and Management*. Vol. 45, January-February 1971.

Beechy, T. H. "The Cost of Leasing: Comment and Correction." *The Accounting Review*. October 1970.

Beechy, T. H. "Quasi-Debt Analysis of Financial Leases." *The Accounting Review*. April 1969.

Bower, R. S., F. D. Herringer and J. P. Williamson. "Lease Evaluation." *The Accounting Review*. April 1966.

Chambers, J., S. Mullick and P. Weekes. "Lease-Buy Planning Decisions." *Management Science*. Vol. 15:6, February 1969.

Doenges, C. R. "The Cost of Leasing." *The Engineering Economist*. Fall 1971.

Ferrara, W. L. "Capital Budgeting and Financing or Leasing Decisions." *Management Accounting* (NAA). July 1968.

Ferrara, W. L. "Lease vs. Purchase: A Quasi-Financing Approach." *Management Accounting* (NAA). January 1974.

Johnson, R. W. and W. Lewellen. "Analysis of the Lease-or-Buy Decision." *The Journal of Finance*. September 1972.

Gordon, M. "A General Solution to the Buy or Lease Decision: A Pedagogical Note." *The Journal of Finance*. March 1974.

Mitchell, G. B. "After Tax Cost of Leasing." *The Accounting Review*. April 1970.

Starbuck, W. "Economic Comparison for Engineering Projects." *Journal of Industrial Engineering*. July-August 1958.

Taylor, D. "Technological or Economic Obsolescences: Computer Purchase vs. Lease." *Management Accounting* (NAA). September 1968.

Wagner, W. "Truck Leasing Analysis." *Journal of Purchasing*. Vol. 7, November 1971.

Wilhelm, M. "Purchase or Lease: That Is the Question." *Management Accounting* (NAA). July 1969.

Make-Buy Decision

Introduction

There are several methods of approach indicated in the literature for dealing with the make-buy decision. Among these, two techniques seem to be most popular. The first is to compare the estimated incremental operating costs of make-or-buy, where these costs are considered to remain constant over time. This approach usually does not consider the time value of money nor does it consider the implicit costs associated with the decision—e.g.,opportunity costs related to the revenues foregone by utilizing existing plant facilities, costs associated with the need for larger inventories, and costs associated with the need for additional working capital.

The second technique, on the other hand, takes into account all incremental costs —e.g.,operating costs, capital expenditures and implicit costs —on a discounted cash flow basis. Since this latter method generally is viewed as the theoretically correct approach, our model is of this type.

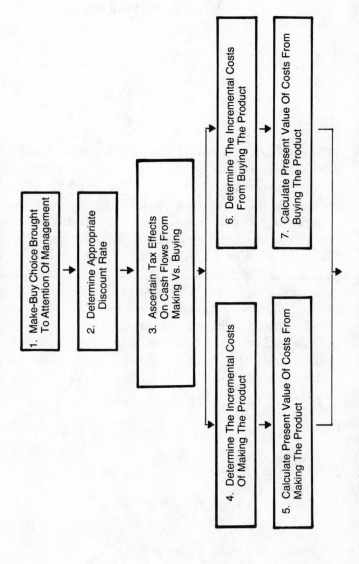

**NORMATIVE MODEL OF
MAKE-BUY DECISION**

(DISCOUNTED CASH FLOW ANALYSIS)

1. Make-Buy Choice Brought To Attention Of Management

2. Determine Appropriate Discount Rate

3. Ascertain Tax Effects On Cash Flows From Making Vs. Buying

4. Determine The Incremental Costs Of Making The Product

5. Calculate Present Value Of Costs From Making The Product

6. Determine The Incremental Costs From Buying The Product

7. Calculate Present Value Of Costs From Buying The Product

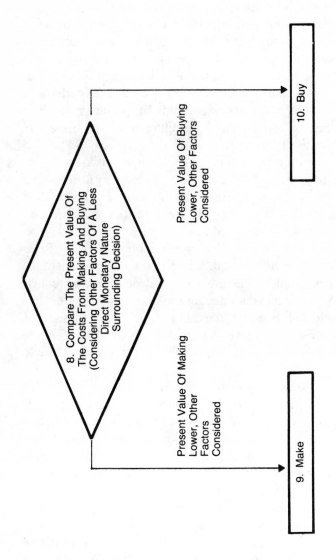

8. Compare The Present Value Of The Costs From Making And Buying (Considering Other Factors Of A Less Direct Monetary Nature Surrounding Decision)

Present Value Of Buying Lower, Other Factors Considered

Present Value Of Making Lower, Other Factors Considered

10. Buy

9. Make

Elaboration on the Flowchart

1. *Make-Buy choice brought to the attention of management.* The make-buy choice situation is brought to the attention of management. It may take several forms. For example, the decision might be to make or buy a product the firm is not currently making or buying; it may be to *continue to make* or begin purchasing an item; or it may be to *continue to buy* or begin to manufacture an item. If the required capital investment to make the product is large, it is particularly important to view the decision as a capital budgeting decision in which discounted cash flows and opportunity costs of capital are considered. The present value (PV) method (see discussion on Capital Expenditure Decision) usually is advocated for this process.

2. *Determine appropriate discount rate.* When the discounted cash flow method is used for make-buy decisions, it is necessary to determine the appropriate discount rate for use in the discounting process. (See Capital Expenditure Decision, step 11, for a further discussion on determining the appropriate discount rate.)

3. *Ascertain tax effects on cash flows from making vs. buying.* Taxes are a key, and often underemphasized, factor in comparing the merits of make and buy. For example, if the firm makes instead of buys a product, it must often buy plant and equipment in order to do so. These items result in depreciation which affects the cash outflows via the amount of taxes. Any other considerations which stem from tax regulations should be taken into account (e.g., the impact of early retirement due to obsolescence).

4 and 6. *Determine the incremental costs from making vs. buying.* If we assume that the selling price of the product is the same whether it is made or bought, the firm need look only at the costs of the make and buy alternatives. Examples of costs which may pertain specifically to the make alternative are investment in new equipment, revenues foregone by utilizing existing plant facilities, and incremental amounts of factory overhead (e.g., how would lighting, heating and indirect labor be affected). Costs which are important in looking at the buy decision include the costs associated with the additional inventories which may be required to be kept on hand to serve as a buffer. (This may not be necessitated under the make alternative where the firm has more control over the factors of production.) In summary, the key point is to consider all incremental costs for each alternative, including opportunity costs, for a number of periods into the future. (For a detailed list of those costs

which are often important in the "make-or-buy" decision of manufacturing firms, see the NAA's MAP Statement No. 5, pp. 7-12.)

5 and 7. *Calculate the present value of costs from the make and buy alternatives*. An orderly way to set up this calculation is to take the number of periods deemed relevant to the project (often set equal to the expected economic life of the equipment to be purchased) and for each period estimate the costs, in terms of net cash outflows, pertaining to the project under each alternative. The net cash outflows, under each alternative, could be discounted using the following equation:

$$\text{Present Value} = \sum_{i=1}^{n} \frac{R_i}{(1+K)^i}$$

where R_i is the net cash outflow for period i (which would consider any salvage value from capital investments made under the make alternative), K is the discount rate, and n is the number of periods under consideration.

8. *Compare the PV of the costs from making to that of buying*. If the PV of the costs of making is less than that of buying, then the direct monetary implication is that it will cost the company less to make the product than to buy it, and thus the product should be produced internally. Alternatively, if the PV of the costs of buying is less than that of making, then buying is cheaper and thus the preferred decision. However, nonfinancial factors which influence the make or buy alternative also must be examined. If the *make* alternative is cheaper, the analyst should examine whether there is much risk of equipment becoming obsolete. A firm could be severely prejudiced against the make alternative if high risk is considered to be present. The firm's areas of competence also may have to be examined to determine if the product to be produced can be manufactured and sold as a high quality item. Outside manufacturers might have more experience and may be prone to making a better product. Another factor which might negate the value of the make alternative would be the impact of making on the computation of financial ratios (e.g., the firm's ROI will be affected by the increased asset base where new facilities are needed to make the product). Some *value judgments* will have to be made to determine whether to go ahead with the chosen alternative or to re-evaluate the situation.

If the buy alternative appears better, again an examination of non-financial factors should be considered as a final selection exercise for determining the course of action to be taken. Some key factors which may enter the picture when the buy alternative is chosen are the foregone advantages of vertical integration, such as steady sources of supply and better control over product attributes. Also, if the firm decides to stop making the product, it must ascertain whether it could get rid of the excess manpower or allocate it effectively to other tasks without generating costly labor-management friction. (For further discussion on the non-financial consideration of the make-buy decision, the reader is referred to MAP Statement No. 5, pp. 15-18.)

9–10. These are action steps which follow from the analysis.

BIBLIOGRAPHY

Doney, L. "Coping with Uncertainty in the Make or Buy Decision." *Management Accounting* (NAA). October 1968.

Fisher, A. and D. Raunick. "A Probabilistic Make-Buy Model." *Journal of Purchasing*. Vol. 8, February 1972.

Friedman, I. *Cost Controls and Profit Improvement Through Product Analysis*. Englewood Cliffs, N.J.: Prentice-Hall, 1966.

Galbraith, O. and J. Morese. "Hire or Overtime: A Best Bet Method." *Management Accounting* (NAA). July 1972.

Gross, H. "Make or Buy Decisions in Growing Firms." *Accounting Review*. Vol. 41, October 1966.

Gross, H. *Make or Buy*, Englewood Cliffs, N.J.: Prentice-Hall, 1966.

Gross, I. "Purchasing Decisions under Conditions of Uncertainty." *Journal of Purchasing*. November 1966.

Horngren, C. *Accounting for Management Control*. Chapter 13, Second Edition, Englewood Cliffs, N.J.: Prentice-Hall, 1970.

Keller, I. W. and W. Ferrara. "Decision Making and the Accountant." in author's *Management Accounting for Profit Control*. Second Edition, New York: McGraw-Hill, 1966.

Lundgren, E. and J. Schneider, "Marginal Cost Model for the Hiring-Overtime Decision." *Management Science*. Vol. 17:6, February 1971.

Lyall, D. "Can We Really Assess Consultants?" *The Accountant's Magazine*. April 1972.

Mitchell, G. "The Make or Buy Decision—A Case Study." *Management Accounting* (NAA). November 1967.

National Association of Accountants. MAP Statement No. 5, *Criteria for Make-or-Buy Decisions*. June 1973.

Newton, D. "Advertising Agency Services—Make or Buy?" *Harvard Business Review*. Vol. 43:4, July-August 1965.

Niland, P. "Make or Buy Special Automatic Equipment?" in author's *Management Problems in Acquisition of Special Automatic Equipment*. 1961.

Schiff, M. and S. Arbesfeld. "Goodwill—A Make or Buy Approach." *Management Accounting* (NAA). August 1966.

Shore, B. "Quantitative Analysis and the Make or Buy Decision." *Journal of Purchasing*. Vol. 6, February 1970.

Ward, E. "Making the Proper Make-or-Buy Decision." *NAA Bulletin*. January 1964.

Pricing Decision

Introduction

The bulk of the normative literature on the pricing decision is economics oriented, where the firm's pricing objective is to maximize profits by setting marginal revenue equal to marginal cost. However, the accounting-oriented literature on profit planning, where the firm's pricing objective is usually to derive an acceptable rate of return on investment, also has direct implications for the pricing decision. In fact, one could argue that profit planning is really a sub-problem of the pricing decision (a cogent argument for the reverse also could be made). Our flowchart brings together the two discussions.

Most discussions of the pricing decision differentiate between variable and fixed costs. For example, in the economics-oriented literature, the short-run pricing decision is a function of only variable costs, thereby ignoring fixed costs. Furthermore, since by definition fixed costs do not exist in the long run, the long-run pricing decision again only has variable costs to consider. This time, however, the variable costs are of a long-run nature. Thus, a short-run pricing decision may differ from a long-run pricing decision due to the differences between short- and long-run variable costs.

The accounting-oriented literature, on the other hand, usually considers all costs (variable and fixed) in determining a product's short-run price. In other words, costs for short-run pricing decisions and costs for long-run pricing decisions usually are considered to be one in the same. The argument often made in defense of this approach is that all costs (total costs) must be covered in the long run, and thus fixed costs cannot be ignored. Some departure from this rule has, however, occurred in the accounting literature where a contribution margin approach to short-run pricing has been advocated.

Our model presented here assumes that a long-run view of the pricing decision is being taken. Thus, in the economics-oriented part of the model, where profit maximization is the pricing objective, marginal costs are considered to be derived from long-run total (which are all variable) costs. In the accounting-oriented part of the model, where an

NORMATIVE MODEL OF
PRICING DECISION

1. Determine Market Environment Of Firm

3. Forecast Product's Demand Curve And Derive Its Revenue Function

2. Estimate Product's Cost Structure

4. Determine Pricing Objective

Acceptable Rate of Return

Profit Maximization

6. Determine Acceptable Return On Investment (ROI)

7. Calculate Income Required To Achieve Target ROI

5. Determine Price And Output At Which Marginal Cost Equals Marginal Revenue

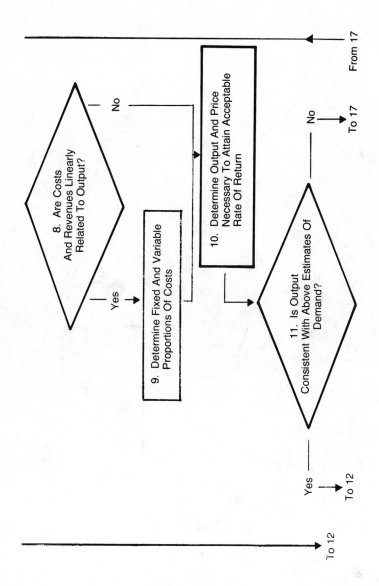

8. Are Costs And Revenues Linearly Related To Output?

No

9. Determine Fixed And Variable Proportions Of Costs

Yes

10. Determine Output And Price Necessary To Attain Acceptable Rate Of Return

11. Is Output Consistent With Above Estimates Of Demand?

No → To 17

Yes → To 12

From 17

To 12

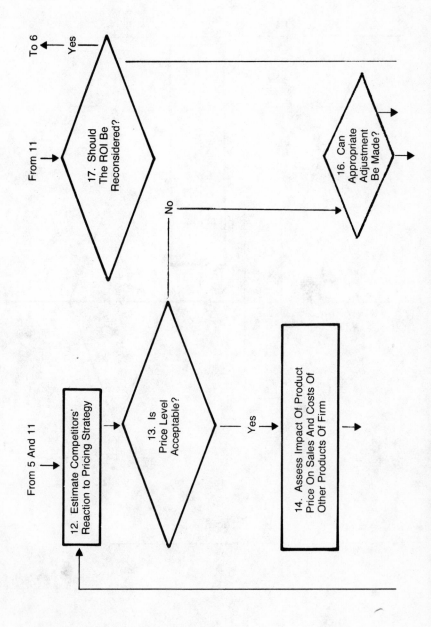

To 6

Yes

From 11

17. Should The ROI Be Reconsidered?

16. Can Appropriate Adjustment Be Made?

No

From 5 And 11

12. Estimate Competitors' Reaction to Pricing Strategy

13. Is Price Level Acceptable?

Yes

14. Assess Impact Of Product Price On Sales And Costs Of Other Products Of Firm

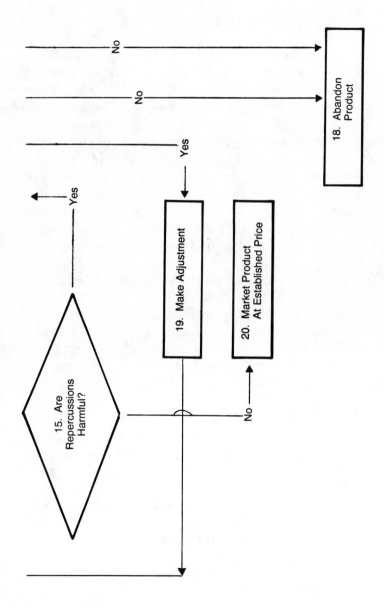

No

No

Yes

18. Abandon Product

Yes

19. Make Adjustment

20. Market Product At Established Price

15. Are Repercussions Harmful?

No

87

acceptable rate of return on investment is the pricing objective, total costs (which are considered to be composed of short-run variable and fixed costs) are utilized in determining the firm's pricing decision.

Elaboration on the Flowchart

1. *Determine market environment of firm.* In setting the price of its product, a firm must first attempt to discover its market environment. Fundamentally there are four types of markets in which a product may be sold. They are: (a) pure competition, (b) monopoly, (c) oligopoly, and (d) monopolistic competition. Determining the type of market which applies to a product can be accomplished by: (1) establishing the number of competitors and their respective share of the market, (2) examining the similarites of competing products with own product and (3) discovering the nature of price competition (e.g., price cutting or product differentiation and promotion) in the product's market. The ease of entry of new firms into the market and the mobility of resources used in production may also help in assessing the product's market environment.

2. *Estimate the cost structure of the product.* Estimating the product's cost structure can be achieved by consulting the cost and output figures available from sources within the firm (e.g., production records, supplier invoices and estimates, costing studies). Econometric studies also may be used to this end, especially where costs are a function of several input variables. When costs are common to more than one product produced by the firm, special care must be given to assure a proper allocation scheme.

3. *Forecast product's demand curve and derive its revenue function.* Estimating the demand for a product seems to be more of an art than a science. Several factors will, however, affect a product's demand and should be considered. Among these factors are: (1) the product's price, (2) the company's advertising policy, (3) the number and closeness of substitutes for the product, and (4) the overall economic outlook for the economy and industry in which the product is sold. Once a product's demand curve has been estimated, its revenue function can be determined.

Several forecasting methods which are often advocated as an aid to determining a product's demand curve are: simple extrapolation of past demand, econometric studies and opinion polls. Accounting records may be able to help in the forecasting process by providing pertinent historical data. Wherever possible, however, changes in the future demand which are discontinuous with the past should be considered (e.g., production and R & D departments may be able to provide valuable information on technological trends).

4. *Determine pricing objective.* Company policies should be examined to determine pricing objectives. Such policies might be found in manuals or through interviews with top executives. The two most common pricing objectives are: (1) maximize profits, which usually is associated with the economics-oriented literature, and (2) determine acceptable rate of return on investment, which usually is associated with the accounting-oriented literature. Many managers think they are pursuing one pricing policy when, in fact, they are pursuing another or some combination of policies. Thus, careful analysis often is needed in clarifying the pricing objective.

5. *Determine price and output required for profit maximization.* From a theoretical point of view, maximization of profits requires the setting of marginal revenue equal to marginal cost. The production necessary to attain this objective can be determined from the cost and revenue functions derived in steps 2 and 3.

6. *Determine acceptable return on investment (ROI).* Determining the firm's acceptable rate of return can be achieved by investigating corporate policies on investments and/or rates of return for other firms in the industry. Returns on investments often are computed on total assets or on stockholders' equity.

7. *Calculate the required income to achieve the target ROI.* A firm's target ROI can be expressed as follows: ROI = Income from Operations ÷ Average Invested Capital, where ROI and Invested Capital are given. From this equation, the income necessary to achieve a certain ROI is easily determined by multiplying the ROI by the Average Invested Capital.

8. *Determine whether costs and revenues are linearly related to output.* Whether costs and revenues are linearly related to output can be determined by using information gathered in steps 2 and 3.

9. *Determine fixed and variable proportions of costs.* If costs are linearly related to output (at least in the relevant range of the firm's operations), then the portion related to variable costs is a constant amount per unit. This amount can be used in determining the product's contribution margin per unit needed in step 10. Regression analysis may be a useful technique in separating costs which are partly fixed and partly variable.

10. *Find the output and price necessary to attain an acceptable rate*

of return. When costs and revenues are linear with respect to output, the output necessary to attain the target income (before taxes) can be determined using the following equation:

$$\frac{\text{Fixed Costs} + \text{Profits}}{\text{Contribution Margin per unit}}$$

When costs and/or revenues are not linear with respect to output, it will be necessary to examine the total cost and revenue functions (derived in steps 2 and 3) to determine the necessary level of production to obtain the target income level.

11. *Determine whether price and output arrived at are consistent with demand studies*. The firm must determine if the output and price calculated in step 10 agree with the demand curve estimated in step 3. Since any derivation of the demand function should be thought of as an estimate, the concern here should be with the feasibility of selling within a desired range of output at a given price rather than with an exact price-output relationship.

12–13. *Estimate the probable reaction of competitors to pricing strategy*. Before a firm actually starts to sell the product at the derived price, the competitors' reactions to past pricing strategies should be examined. For example, if the established price is going to set off a price war, then it may be wise to reconsider the price.

14–15. *Assess the impact of the product's price on sales and costs of other products sold by the firm*. Production costs of one product may be interrelated to the costs of another product. Also, the demand for one product may be partly or wholly dependent on the demand of another product made by the firm. For example, a company producing cameras and film would want to consider the impact of selling more cameras upon the demand for film. If the repercussions on other company products are harmful, then the product's pricing strategy must be reconsidered. Past experience, expert opinions, cross elasticity studies and joint cost studies are among the many ways to assess the impact of a product's price on the sales and costs of other products sold by the firm.

16. *Can appropriate adjustment be made?* If the pricing strategy of the product is expected to create problems with competitors and/or with other products of the firm, then an appropriate adjustment must be considered. Where a major adjustment is required, the firm may have to re-evaluate the pricing objective of the product.

17. *Should the ROI be reconsidered?* If estimates of demand are not

consistent with the determined price and output required to meet the company's pricing objective, it may be necessary to revise downward the company's target ROI. Also, as mentioned in step 16, if problems with competitors and/or other products of the company result from the product's pricing strategy, it may be necessary to reconsider the company's target ROI. Company policy and/or the opinions of executives may shed some light on this step.

18–20. These are action steps which follow from the analysis.

BIBLIOGRAPHY

Abacus, J. "A New Model for Testing Pricing Decisions." *Journal of Marketing*. Vol. 28:3, July 1964.

Arnold, J. "On the Problem of Internal Pricing Decisions." *Accounting and Business Research*. Vol. 3, Spring 1973.

Barker, R. "Decision Model in Consumer Pricing Research." *Journal of Marketing Research*. Vol. 9, August 1972.

Braverman, J. "Decision Theoretic Approach to Pricing." *Decision Sciences*. Vol. 2, January 1971.

Burck, G. "The Myths and Realities of Corporate Pricing." *Fortune,* April 1972.

Colantoni, C., R. Manes and A. Whinston. "Programming, Profits Rates and Pricing Decisions." *Accounting Review*. Vol.44, July 1969.

Cutler, G. "Developing the Selling Price." *Management Accounting* (NAA). August 1971.

Darden, B. "Operational Approach to Product Pricing." *Journal of Marketing*. Vol. 32:2, April 1968.

Fama, E. "Perfect Competition and Optimal Production Decisions Under Uncertainty." *Bell Journal of Economics and Management Science*. Vol. 3, Autumn 1972.

Finerty, J. "Product Pricing and Investment Analysis." *Management Accounting* (NAA). December 1971.

Flower, J. "A Risk Analysis Approach to Marginal Cost Pricing." *Accounting and Business Research*. Vol. 1, Autumn 1971.

Frederick, D. "Industrial Pricing Decision Using Bayesian Multivariable Analysis." *Journal of Marketing Research*. Vol. 8, May 1971.

Green, P. "Bayesian Decision Theory in Pricing Strategy." *Journal of Marketing*. Vol. 27:1, January 1963.

Hinkle, C. "The Strategy of Price Deals." *Harvard Business Review*. Vol. 43:4, July-August 1965.

Joskow, P. "Pricing Decisions of Regulated Firms: a Behavioral Approach," *Bell Journal of Economics and Management Science*. Vol. 4:1, Spring 1973.

Kallimanis, W. "Product Contribution Analysis for Multi-Product Pricing." *Management Accounting* (NAA). June 1968.

Knox, R. "Competitive Oligopolistic Pricing." *Journal of Marketing*. Vol. 30:3, July 1966.

Lynn, R. and D. Rogoff. "Methods vs. Objectives in Pricing Policy." *Management Advisor*. March-April 1972.

Miller, D. and M. Starr. *Executive Decisions and Operations Research*. Second Edition. Englewood Cliffs, N.J.: Prentice-Hall, 1969.

Newman, R. "A Game Theory Approach to Competitive Bidding." *Journal of Purchasing*. Vol. 8, February 1972.

Newman, R. "Analysis of Competitive Bidding Strategy." *Journal of Purchasing*. May 1967.

Oxenfeldt, A. "A Decision Making Structure for Price Decisions." *Journal of Marketing*. Vol. 37: 1, January 1973.

Oxenfeldt, A. "Product Line Pricing." *Harvard Business Review*. July-August 1966.

Palda, K. *Pricing Decisions and Marketing Policy*. Englewood Cliffs, N.J.: Prentice-Hall, 1971.

Riley, W. "Financial Responsibility and Sales Prices." *Management Accounting* (NAA). September 1967.

Rutenberg, D. "Three Pricing Policies for a Multi-Product, Multi-National Company." *Management Science*. Vol. 17:8, April 1971.

Sanju-Shibata. "How to Choose Profitable Orders in Jobbing Firms." *Journal of Industrial Engineering*. Annual Proceedings 21, 1970.

Sampson, R.T. "Sense and Sensitivity in Pricing." *Harvard Business Review*. November-December 1964.

Simmonds, K. "Competitive Bidding: Deciding the Best Combination of Non-Price Features." *Operations Research Quarterly*. March 1968.

Slater, C. and F. Mossman. "Positive Robinson-Patman Pricing." *Journal of Marketing*. April 1967.

Smidt S. "Flexible Pricing of Computer Services." *Management Science*. Vol. 14:10, June 1968.

Stark R. "Competitive Bidding: a Comprehensive Bibliography." *Operations Research*. March 1971.

Twedt, D. "How to Plan New Products, Improve Old Ones, and Create Better Advertising." *Journal of Marketing*. Vol. 33:1, January 1969.

Walter, A. "How to Price Industrial Products." *Harvard Business Review*. September-October 1967.

Wentz, T. "Realism in Pricing Analyses." *Journal of Marketing*. April 1966.

Manpower Planning Decision

Introduction

Textbooks on personnel management seem to place much more emphasis on the derived decisions of manpower planning, such as recruitment, selection, and wage and salary administration, than they do on the overall manpower planning process. The general tendency of the literature which does discuss manpower planning is to focus upon the information required to establish manpower needs. Unfortunately, little attention is paid to the procedural aspects of setting up a system to gather and analyze such information. Our chart has been compiled by taking into account the information requirements cited in the literature and structuring the order in which they must be considered according to the logic implied by authors writing about the process.

The Personnel Recruitment Decision is shown as an appendix of the Manpower Planning Decision.

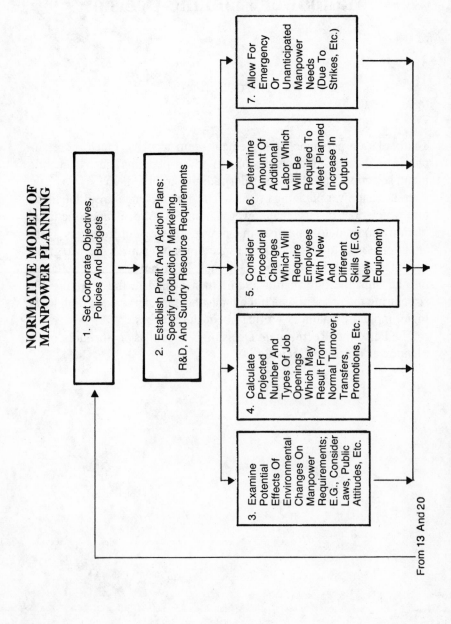

NORMATIVE MODEL OF MANPOWER PLANNING

1. Set Corporate Objectives, Policies And Budgets

2. Establish Profit And Action Plans: Specify Production, Marketing, R&D, And Sundry Resource Requirements

3. Examine Potential Effects Of Environmental Changes On Manpower Requirements; E.G., Consider Laws, Public Attitudes, Etc.

4. Calculate Projected Number And Types Of Job Openings Which May Result From Normal Turnover, Transfers, Promotions, Etc.

5. Consider Procedural Changes Which Will Require Employees With New And Different Skills (E.G., New Equipment)

6. Determine Amount Of Additional Labor Which Will Be Required To Meet Planned Increase In Output

7. Allow For Emergency Or Unanticipated Manpower Needs (Due To Strikes, Etc.)

From 13 And 20

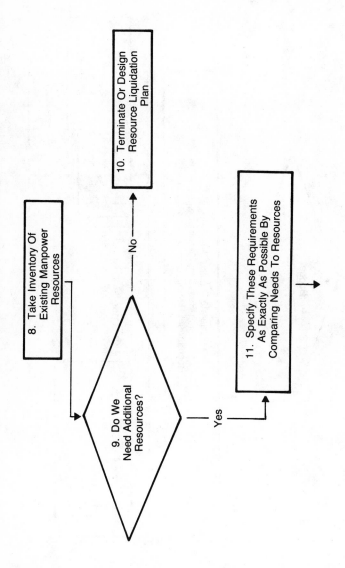

97

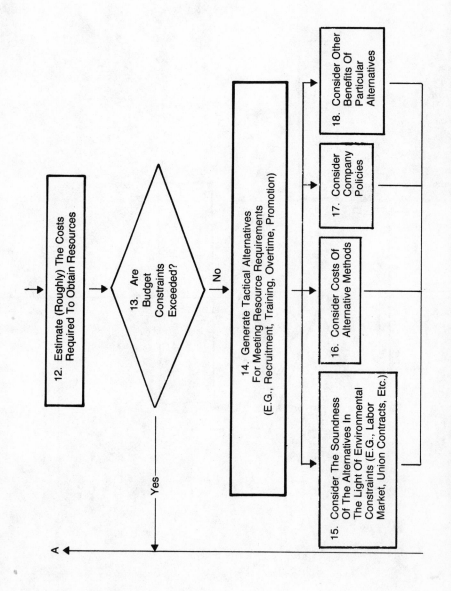

12. Estimate (Roughly) The Costs Required To Obtain Resources

13. Are Budget Constraints Exceeded?

Yes

No

A

14. Generate Tactical Alternatives For Meeting Resource Requirements (E.G., Recruitment, Training, Overtime, Promotion)

15. Consider The Soundness Of The Alternatives In The Light Of Environmental Constraints (E.G., Labor Market, Union Contracts, Etc.)

16. Consider Costs Of Alternative Methods

17. Consider Company Policies

18. Consider Other Benefits Of Particular Alternatives

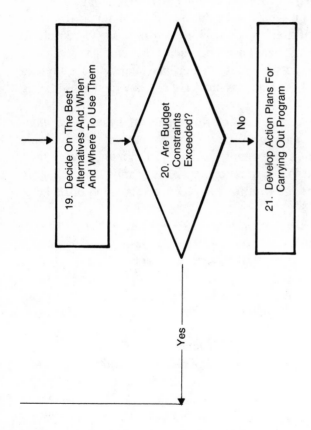

19. Decide On The Best Alternatives And When And Where To Use Them

20. Are Budget Constraints Exceeded?

No

21. Develop Action Plans For Carrying Out Program

Yes

99

Elaboration on the Flowchart

1. *Set corporate objectives, policies and budgets.* Manpower planning is to a large extent a function of organizational constraints and goals. Thus it is wise to have a clear conception of what these are before proceeding with the planning task. An example of the interaction between planning of manpower requirements and organizational policies and budgets is easy to demonstrate. Financial resource restrictions occasion the need for some austerity in filling manpower requirements. On the other hand, objectives or policies which strive towards growth usually point to the need for more people and skill types. Each of these forces must influence the staffing process.

2. *Establish specific profit and action plans.* While objectives and policies give a rough idea of the types and quantities of human resources required, more specific information is needed in order to be able to adequately staff the organization. Departmental action plans result in a better idea of the basic resources (human and material) required to achieve objectives. These plans should serve as a key input in assessing manpower requirements.

3. *Examine potential effects of environmental changes on manpower needs.* Legal and social developments can affect the firm's staffing requirements. For example, changes in minimum wage laws may make it more desirable to automate. Bans against discriminatory practices may require the firm to change the composition of its labor force.

4. *Calculate the projected number of job openings which may result from turnover, transfers, etc.* and specify the types of openings which are likely to occur and the skill requirements necessary to fill them. Information on the number of employees which will have to be replaced due to such attrition is available in the form of past experience, economic projections (the better the labor market, the higher the turnover), etc.

5. *Consider procedural changes* which will require employees possessing new and different skills. If action plans call for the introduction of new types of technology, new types of skills will be required of personnel. This fact should be reflected in the overall assessment of manpower resource requirements. The production and industrial engineering departments should be able to provide information regarding the specific skills required.

6. *Determine additional labor which will be required to meet action plans.* If plans specify new product lines or increased outputs or ac-

tivities for the coming time interval, additional labor requirements must be calculated. This could be achieved using industrial engineering standards for similar jobs which specify how much a given employee is capable of producing given his skills.

7. *Allow for slack or special inputs into the manpower requirement considerations to cope with unanticipated needs or emergencies.* Events such as strikes, unexpected jumps in demand for products, and so forth, may require the firm to obtain manpower quickly. There are two basic means of coping with such situations. The first is to keep on hand a reserve of manpower. This, of course, is costly. An alternative tactic is to try to adapt as quickly as possible to the new situation by importing (or developing) the required skills into the company. Here, there is a chance that adaption will be slow and opportunities will be missed. These matters must be decided by looking at the environments closely and taking into account relevant aspects of company policy.

8. *Take inventory of existing manpower resources.* Using the records and files maintained in the personnel department, assess the manpower resources currently available to the organization. Electronic data processing systems which store and classify personnel records according to a number of factors (age, skills, department, seniority) are very useful for arriving at such inventories.

9. *Compare manpower needs* arrived at in steps 2, 3, 4, 5, 6 and 7 to manpower *available currently* within the firm. Again, computerized record-keeping can be very valuable in determining the quantity and nature of human resources required by the firm. If no additional resources are required, go to step 10. If some staffing needs remain unfulfilled, proceed to step 11.

10. If manpower on hand exceeds in quantity or capacity (i.e. skills and training) that required in the foreseeable future, it might be useful to *consider getting rid of some personnel* in order to conserve resources. Policy decisions must be made to determine appropriate procedures. Action plans then can be designed. Often it is easiest to use the device of attrition in reducing complements. This keeps morale high and keeps the company relatively free of union-management friction.

11. If there is a shortage of manpower resources, an *inventory should be compiled of the exact requirements* of the firm. Precise specification of staffing needs may be derived from the individual departments requiring the manpower, the industrial engineering department, action plans submitted by departments, information about present job incumbents who hold positions similar to those vacant, etc.

12. *Prepare rough cost estimates of manpower resources* which

must be procured. An examination of current market prices for the types of skills needed and a perusal of relevant job descriptions and associated salary grades should go a long way in determining costs.

13. *Check to see if cost estimates substantially exceed the available budgeted funds*. If not, go to step 14. If so, a reconsideration of original objectives and/or budgets may be required (go to step 1).

14. *Generate tactical alternatives* for attempting to meet staffing requirements. Hiring people is not the only way for the firm to acquire needed resources. Training programs, increased mechanization, promotions, transfers, and having the staff work overtime may all be viable alternatives.

15. The merits of each alternative should be considered in view of union constraints, the nature of the labor market, and other considerations which characterize the *firm's environment*. For example, unions may not permit much overtime or may have so much influence over promotion (via the seniority clause) that some alternatives will prove unfeasible. Similarly, the labor market may not contain persons with requisite skills so that the firm is in effect forced to train its own personnel to fill key vacancies.

16. *Consider costs of alternative methods*. Management must elect from the number of feasible alternatives those which achieve the most at the least cost. Costs may be determined by looking at expense records (past experience) or commissioning special cost studies of the alternatives involved.

17. *Consider company policy*. There are certain alternatives which may be unacceptable in the light of the firm's personnel policies. For instance, the firm may wish to keep a fairly stable labor force so may be averse to fluctuations in the number of employees. In such a case, it might be best to deal with temporary increases in demand by having the staff work overtime rather than temporarily hiring personnel.

18. *Consider sundry benefits of alternatives*. There may be particular advantages to certain alternatives in the light of the objectives and competences of the firm. For example, a number of persons may be available on staff who are extremely competent as trainers of personnel. This fact might argue in favor of training persons who are already members of the organization rather than hiring new persons who already possess the requisite skills.

19. *Decide on the best alternative(s)* and when and where to use each. Steps 15–18 will help determine the most favorable alternatives. They also should help establish when and where each can be used in meeting staffing requirements. Past experience and meetings of func-

tional experts (considering each individual department's needs at each meeting) can help choose the appropriate alternative.

20. Determine whether the *budgetary constraints* are exceeded. If so, go to step 1 and redefine budgets or adjust objectives. If not, proceed to step 21.

21. With the help of recruitment, training and wage and salary experts, *design a plan for implementing the programs devised* in step 19. An example of one way of handling an aspect of this program—the recruitment decision—is attached.

Appendix to Manpower Planning Decision

Personnel Recruitment Decision

Introduction

Articles dealing with how to recruit personnel seem to lend themselves to classification into two similar but basic types. The first looks at recruitment decisions as solely a function of the personnel department. The focus here is on finding the right person for a specific job. Individual candidates' attributes are the center of attention. A second approach takes a slightly broader scope in that some emphasis is placed on the establishment of the types and numbers of manpower required in the organization. This was seen to be discernable only via some extensive project which could enlist the aid of operating and other staff groups. Our manpower planning chart deals in part with the second school of articles. Our attention here is limited to the activities which follow once basic manpower planning activities have taken place.

NORMATIVE MODEL OF
PERSONNEL RECRUITMENT DECISION

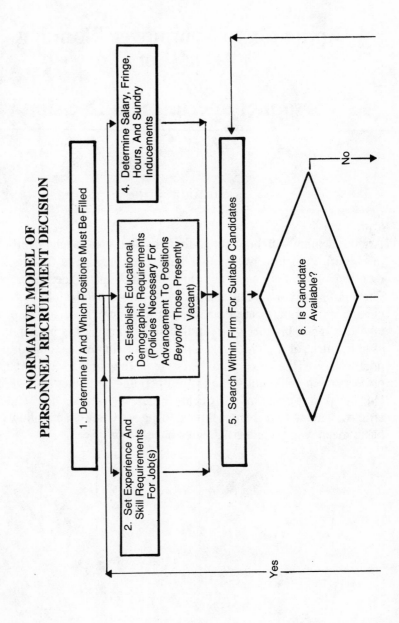

1. Determine If And Which Positions Must Be Filled

2. Set Experience And Skill Requirements For Job(s)

3. Establish Educational, Demographic Requirements (Policies Necessary For Advancement To Positions *Beyond* Those Presently Vacant)

4. Determine Salary, Fringe, Hours, And Sundry Inducements

5. Search Within Firm For Suitable Candidates

6. Is Candidate Available?

Yes

No

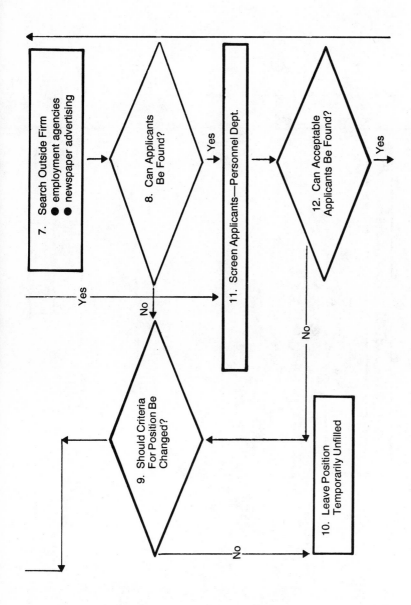

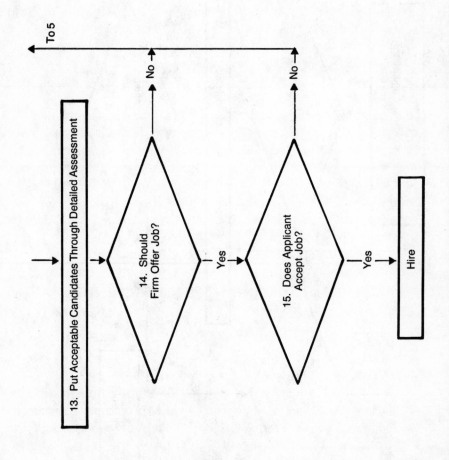

108

Elaboration on the Flowchart

1. Refer to the action plan derived via the manpower planning process in order to *determine which positions must be filled*. It is assumed that increasing overtime and employee training and promotion have been found to be unacceptable alternatives by manpower planners. Transfers of personnel or recruitment of already trained people from outside the firm are viewed as the only possible solutions at this stage.

2–4. While personnel department specialists already have a fair grasp of the employee qualifications required and the nature of the job to be filled, it may be useful to reconsider the position in detail when actually trying to staff it. This is especially true if the job is at a high level or is one which is new and different to the firm. Information on *experience and skill requirements* for the job may be procured from managers of departments who require the manpower. The experience of these persons and their familiarity with the job give them special insights into job requirements. In the interests of obtaining "promotable" personnel, it might be advantageous to view the attributes required of candidates who would be able to progress to managerial posts. Again, inputs from the relevant managers would be helpful. If the position to be filled is a new one, it is important to determine the proper *salary, fringe benefits,* and working conditions which must apply. The personnel department might be guided by information on how other firms treat similar positions.

5–6. *Search for applicants within the firm* who may be able to fill the position by consulting personnel records. It would be ideal if an appropriate employee could be found in a department which has excess complement.

7. If no suitable candidates can be found within the firm, it is time to *examine outside sources of personnel*. Qualified people may be obtained via employment agencies, newspaper or journal advertising, etc. Past experience and a crude cost/benefit analysis may help determine the best way to appeal to outside job candidates.

8–10. If no applicants can be found either within or outside the firm, perhaps *job requirements should be changed*. If this cannot be permitted, the position may have to be left unfilled for a while, and the firm may have to intensify its search or increase the rewards offered to prospective candidates. Budgets and appropriate department managers should be consulted in making these decisions.

11–13. Once applicants are found, they should be *screened* to determine if their aptitudes and qualifications are suitable. This can be accomplished by checking with past employers, examining employment histories, former achievements, transcripts of marks, personnel qualities (via interivew), and so forth. If no suitable candidates can be found, step 9 must be considered since criteria may be unrealistically high. If suitable personnel are available, send them for more *detailed interviews* to their prospective supervisor.

14. If candidates are successful, *offer* them employment.

15. If candidates accept offer, *terminate* process. If not, resume search or screening.

BIBLIOGRAPHY

Allocation/Planning

Ahnoni, A., T. Mahoney and G. Milkovich. "The Use of the Delphi Procedures in Manpower Forecasting." *Management Science*. Vol. 19:4, December 1972.

Andrew, G. and A. Lorents. "Allocation of Buyers' Time to Functional Activities." *Journal of Purchasing*. Vol. 8, November 1972.

Banfield. "Manpower Utilization Planning and Cost Control." *Journal of Industrial Engineering*, Annual Proceedings 20, 1969.

Bassett, G. "Manpower Forecasting and Planning: Problems and Solutions." *Personnel*. Vol. 47, September 1970.

Beem, W. "Building Services—Staff Utilization Program Results." A working paper from Professor Daniel Teichroew, Department of Industrial Engineering, University of Michigan. (Listed as part of bibliography of working papers, *Management Science,* February 1970. Paper dated Nov. 5, 1969.)

Blakely, R. "Markov Models and Manpower Planning." *Industrial Management Review,* Vol. 11:2, Winter 1970.

Brassell-Long, "Aproach to Quantitative Determination of Crew Size." *Journal of Industrial Engineering,* Annual Proceedings 21, 1970.

Childs, M. and H. Wolfe. "A Decision and Value Approach to Research Personnel Allocation." *Management Science*. Vol. 18:6, February 1972.

Cleff, S. and R. Hecht. "Computer Job/Man Matching at Blue Collar Levels." *Personnel*. Vol. 48, January 1971.

Dill, W., D. Gaver, and W. Weber. "Models and Modelling for Manpower Planning." *Management Science*. Vol. 13:4, December 1966.

Jewett, R. "A Minimum Risk Manpower Scheduling Technique." *Management Science,* Vol. 13:10, June 1967.

King, W. "A Stochastic Personnel-Assignment Model." *Operations Research*. Vol. 13, January-February 1965.

Maddox, R. "Problems and Trends in Assigning Managers Overseas." *Personnel*. Vol. 48, January 1971.

Marshall, P. "Implementing a Manpower Inventory System." *Personnel*. Vol. 48:2, March-April 1971.

Nelson, R. "Labor Assignment as a Dynamic Control Problem." *Operations Research,* Vol. 14:3, May-June 1966.

Nemhauser, G. and H. Nuttle. "A Quantitative Approach to Employment Planning." *Management Science.* Vol. 11:10, June 1965.

Nuttle, H. "Application of Dynamic Programming to Employment Planning." *Journal of Industrial Engineering.* Annual Proceedings 20, 1969.

Patz, A. "Linear Programming Applied to Manpower Management." *Industrial Management Review,* Vol. 11:2, Winter 1970.

Townsend, M. "Data Needs for Manpower Planning." *Operations Research Quarterly.* Vol. 19, December 1968.

Wikstrom, W. "Manpower Planning: Evolving Systems." *The Conference Board.* Report #521, 1971.

Willings, D. "Fitting the Man to the Job." *Personnel Management.* Vol. 1, August 1969.

Recruitment/Selection

Clarke, L. "Decision Models for Personnel Selection and Assignment." *Personnel Administration.* Vol. 32, March-April 1969.

Ference, T. "Can Personnel Selection Be Computerized?" *Personnel.* Vol. 45, November 1968.

Gallagher, W. and E. Phelps. "Integrated Approach to Technical Staffing." *Harvard Business Review,* Vol. 41:4, July-August 1963.

Greenlaw, P. and R. Smith. "Simulation of a Psychological Decision Process in Personnel Selection." *Management Science.* Vol. 13:8, April 1967.

Martin, R. "Employment Advertising—Hard Sell, Soft Sell, or What?" *Personnel.* Vol. 48, May 1971.

Moore, M. "Recruiting and Retaining Manufacturing Staff Personnel." *Personnel.* Vol. 46, November 1969.

Appendix A

Appendix A: Three Illustrations of the 'Non-Programmed' Decision Process

The three attached figures show researchers' attempts to describe complex managerial tasks, essentially decision processes that have never been programmed by management scientists. The first derives from Aguilar's work on how managers scan their environments for information. His 16 points describe the following: from undirected viewing, the manager finds an issue and first decides whether he needs more information. If he does not, he makes a decision on the issue. If he does, he assigns one of three modes to his subsequent search procedures as follows. He passively exposes himself to a more or less clearly identified type of information ("conditioned viewing"); he searches in an informal and limited way for information of a specific purpose ("informal search"); or he deliberately and systematically searches for information related to a specific issue ("formal search"). If further information shows the issue to be irrelevant, the manager returns to a fourth mode, "undirected viewing," which Aguilar defines as "general exposure to information where the viewer has no specific purpose in mind with the possible exception of exploration" (1967:19). If this search is unsuccessful or if there is no appropriate search procedure available, the manager goes to a subroutine where he can change his scanning rules.

The second figure shows the scheduling program developed by Radomsky to describe how the managers he studied scheduled their time. He notes the process of scanning new information, switching some of it to other people (together with responsibility for execution of certain tasks), and sequencing remaining tasks. Sequencing of the manager's inventory of known problems is a complex process; according to Radomsky it involves the following implicit rules:

1. Locate the jobs with negative or zero slack or imminent start dates. Arrange in order of lateness penalty sequence.
2. Compare time available to time required for completion. If conflict exists, move obstruction if it has slack. If obstruction has no slack and has high visibility, resolve by assigning completion of project in hand or obstruction to a subordinate.

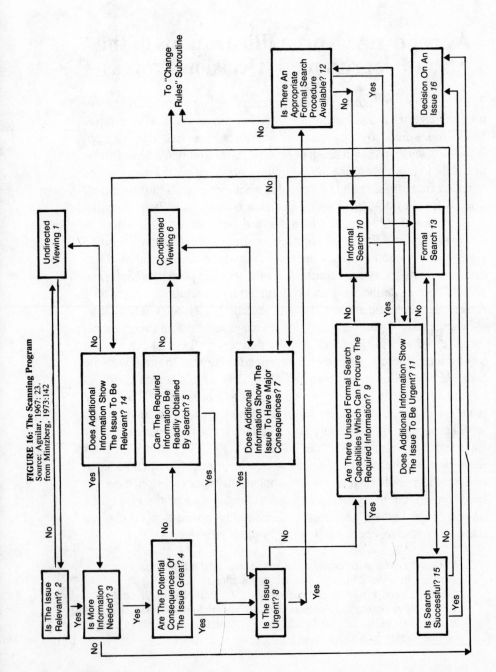

FIGURE 16: The Scanning Program
Source: Aguilar, 1967: 23,
from Mintzberg, 1973:142

116

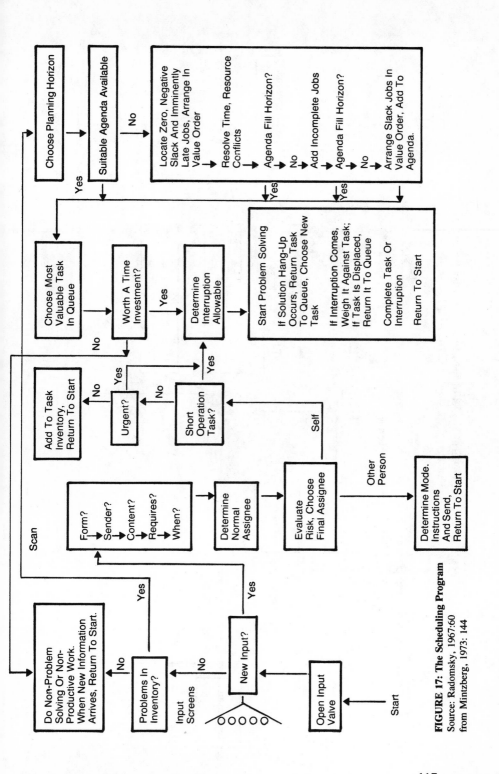

FIGURE 17: The Scheduling Program
Source: Radomsky, 1967:60
from Mintzberg, 1973: 144

117

FIGURE 4: A General Model of the Strategic Decision Process (Mintzberg, Raisinghani, Theoret, 1973)

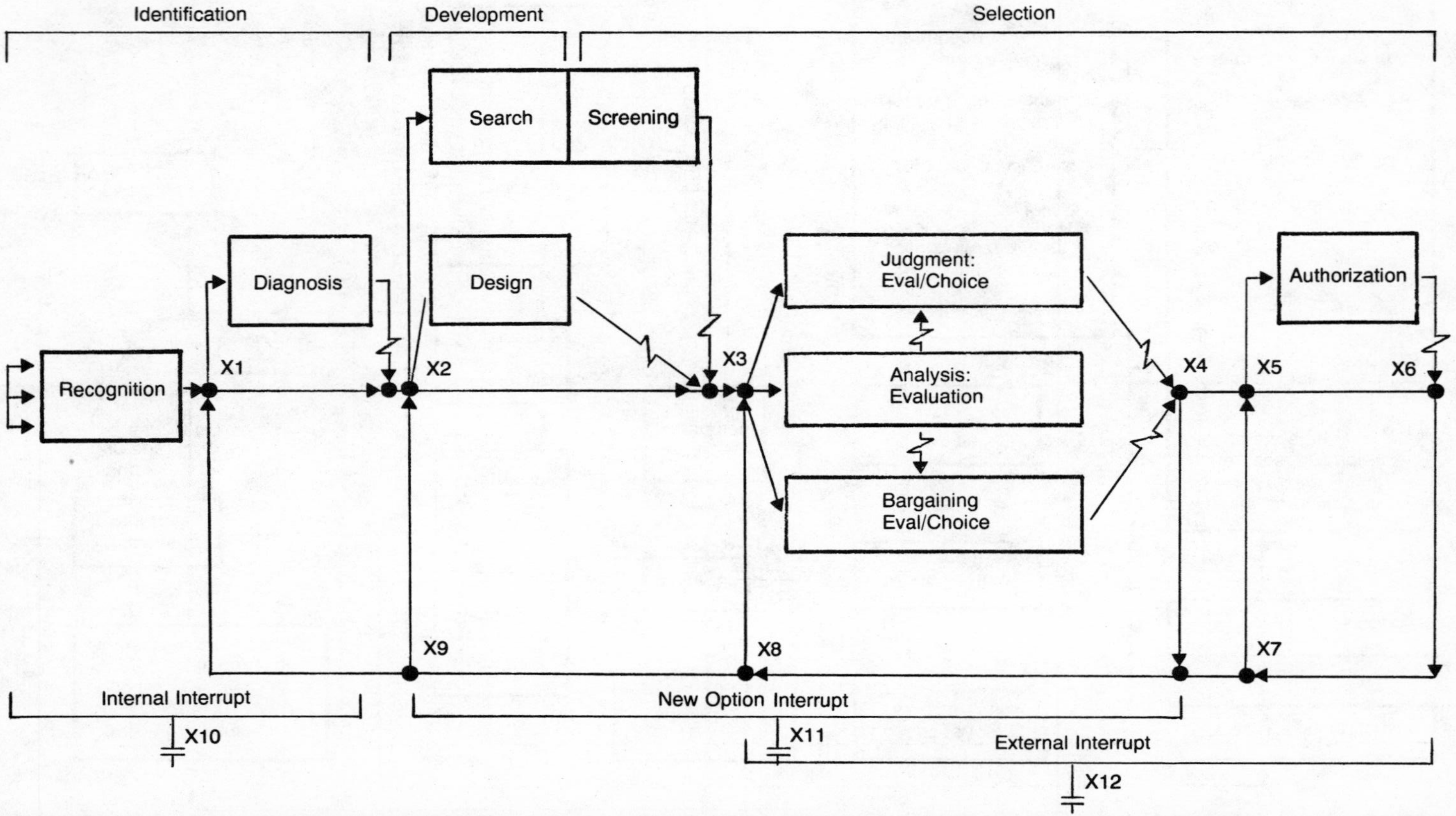

118

3. If no higher class jobs exist, consider completing any partially completed jobs ahead of a new job with slack.
4. Schedule jobs with slack according to priority value. Do not rearrange the fixed obstructions, but choose highest value jobs that will fit the span available.
5. Use short operation tasks as fillers for open spots, to break pace, and to start the day.
6. Whenever working on projects with slack, review new input immediately on a first come—first served basis (1967:52-53).

Mintzberg, Raisinghani and Théoret studied 25 strategic decision processes and developed a description of such processes in terms of 12 elements: the three *central phases* include (1) Identification (comprising Recognition and Diagnosis programs), (2) Development (comprising Search and Design programs), and (3) Selection (comprising Screening, Evaluation/Choice, and Authorization programs). The three sets of *parallel processes* include, (4) Decision Control processes, (5) Communication processes, and (6) Political processes. The *dynamic factors,* key distinguishing features of decision processes that are strategic, include (7) Interrupts, (8) Scheduling Delays, (9) Feedback Delays, (10) Timing Delays and Speedups, (11) Comprehension Cycles, (12) Failure Recycles.

They then describe a model of the strategic decision process shown in the third figure, as follows:

The "main line" through the center of the model shows the two steps that must be a part of any decision process—recognition of the situation and the evaluation/choice of a solution. The three modes of the evaluation/choice program are shown at X_3, with analysis (if that is the form of evaluation) necessarily leading to judgment or bargaining (as the mode for making the choice). In theory, therefore, the most basic decision process involves simply recognizing a *given* solution and then evaluating and choosing it. Needless to say, we encountered no case quite so simple.

Most decision processes involve development activity after recognition. Hence, at X_2, there is a branch off the main line into the search (and screening) program to find a *ready-made* solution or into the design program to develop a *custom-made* solution. In virtually all cases, in fact, development was a nested process; hence, at X_4 the model contains a branch from the evaluative/choice program back to the development phase (at X_9) to initiate another search or design cycle. *Modified* solutions, as noted earlier, first follow one or more search cycles (to find a ready-made solution) and then a series of design cycles (to modify it). In addition to nested development, we also noted the common occurrence of nested selection; hence at X_4 and X_8 we show a loop from the evaluation/choice program back to itself.

Any decision process may or may not involve explicit diagnosis activity (typically after recognition) and authorization (typically after final evaluation/choice). Hence, the model shows branches at X_1 and X_5 which take the process off the main line and then return it there when completed. In addition, authorization may be tiered (hence the loop at X_6 and X_7), and authorization to proceed may be sought after recognition or during the development, resulting in a branch from the authorization program back to development (X_6 and X_9). And there is evidence that occasionally the decison process branches from selection (at X_4 or X_6) all the way back to the diagnosis program (past X_8 and X_9) to allow for reconsideration of the whole decision situation. All of these branches also represent the comprehension cycles (for example, cycling within evaluation/choice at X_4 and X_8) and the failure recycles (from the evaluation/choice program at X_4 or the authorization program at X_6 back to redevelopment at X_9 to modify an unacceptable solution or develop a new one, or back to the evaluation/choice program at X_8 to modify criteria).

Many strategic decision processes involve interrupts of one kind or another. The three most common types are shown in the model. At X_{10} are *internal* (political) interrupts in the identification phase, where there is no agreement on the existence of a decision situation. Such interrupts come from within the organization, and lead to cycling in the recognition program (to resolve the disagreement by bargaining or persuasion), to delays (until the resistance subsides), or to political design (to remove the resistance). At X_{12} are *external* interrupts (constraints or political resistance) during the selection phase, where outside forces block the selection of a fully-developed solution. These interrupts typically lead to modification in the design (to bring it in line with the difficulty encountered), to complete redevelopment of a new solution (if the solution appears to be unacceptable), or to bargaining (to confront the resistance directly). At X_{11} are *new option* interrupts which typically occur late in development or during the evaluation/choice program. These lead the process back to design (to elaborate or modify the new option) or directly to evaluation/choice to select or reject it immediately.

Finally, the model shows an inherent delay (in the form of a broken line) between each of the programs. This reflects the fact that scheduling, feedback, and/or timing delays separate every step in the strategic decision process. The model does not show the parallel processes however (except for bargainig as a model of selection), but as has been made clear above, decision control, communication, and political activities can occur in parallel with any program in the model.

120

BIBLIOGRAPHY

Aguilar, F. J. *Scanning the Business Environment*. New York: Macmillan, 1967.

Radomsky, J. "The Problem of Choosing a Problem." (Cambridge, Mass.: M.I.T. Sloan School of Management, unpublished M.S. thesis) referenced in H. Mintzberg, *The Nature of Managerial Work*. (New York: Harper and Row, 1973).

Mintzberg, H., D. Raisinghani and A. Théoret. *The Structure of "Unstructured" Decision Processes*. Montreal: McGill University, Faculty of Management working paper, 1973.

No. 7578-GB-12.5M-10/75